this book belongs to

T0408296

....

Easy Cooking for Kids

More than 50 fun and easy recipes for children aged 3+

Amanda Grant

Photography by Susan Bell

cico**kidz**

Dedicated to my family

This edition published in 2025 by CICO Books
An imprint of Ryland Peters & Small Ltd

20–21 Jockey's Fields
London WC1R 4BW
www.rylandpeters.com
Email: euregulations@rylandpeters.com

1452 Davis Bugg Road
Warrenton, NC 27589

First published in 2011 as *Cook School* by Ryland
Peters & Small

10 9 8 7 6 5 4 3 2 1

Text © Amanda Grant 2011, 2025
Design, illustrations, and photography © Ryland Peters &
Small 2011, 2025

The author's moral rights have been asserted. All rights
reserved. No part of this publication may be reproduced,
stored in a retrieval system, or transmitted in any form or by
any means, electronic, mechanical, photocopying, or
otherwise, without the prior permission of the publisher.

A CIP record for this book is available from the British Library.
US Library of Congress CIP data has been applied for.

ISBN: 978-1-80065-458-7

Printed in China

Prop and food stylist: Amanda Grant
Photoshoot assistants: Brenda Bishop and Esther Webb
Location researcher: Jess Walton
Designer: Geoff Borin
Senior designers: Iona Hoyle and Emily Breen
Editorial assistant: Danielle Rawlings
Senior editor: Céline Hughes
Indexer: Hilary Bird
Art director: Sally Powell
Creative director: Leslie Harrington
Head of production: Patricia Harrington
Publishing manager: Carmel Edmonds
Publishing director: Alison Starling

The authorised representative in the EEA is
Authorised Rep Compliance Ltd.,
Ground Floor. 71 Lower Baggot Street,
Dublin, D01 P593, Ireland
www.arccompliance.com

notes

- All spoon measurements are level unless otherwise specified.

- Both American (Imperial and US cups) and British (Metric) measurements are included in the recipes for your convenience. It is important to work with one set of measurements and not alternate between the two within a recipe.

- Ovens should be preheated to the specified temperatures. We recommend using an oven thermometer and consulting the maker's handbook for any special instructions. If using a fan-assisted oven, adjust the temperatures according to manufacturer's instructions.

- All eggs are medium (UK) or large (US). It is recommended that free-range eggs be used.

- Recipes containing raw or partially cooked egg, or raw fish or shellfish, should not be served to the very young, very old, anyone with a compromised immune system or pregnant women.

Neither the author nor the publisher can be held responsible for any claim arising out of the information in this book. Always consult your health advisor or doctor if you have any concerns about your child's health or nutrition.

FSC
www.fsc.org
MIX
Paper | Supporting
responsible forestry
FSC® C106563

contents

foreword by Marguerite Patten, CBE

Amanda Grant has written a practical and inspiring cookery book for young children.

Amanda has helped parents by producing excellent books on feeding children. Now she is showing children how to achieve a sense of achievement and pleasure by learning to cook.

The accepted method of teaching children to read is by giving them books, toys and information suitable for their age. This approach is followed here.

Interesting information and suitable recipes are given under the ages of 3–5 years, then 5–7 years and 7–11; in the case of food preparation, physical ability must also be considered.

Parents will be thrilled by the extra skills their children will develop.

Marguerite Patten

introduction

Keep this book somewhere safe and enjoy it! You are about to learn some skills that you can use for the rest of your life. If you start cooking now, you will have lots of fun ahead of you making good food for you and your family and friends.

We all need to eat every day and it is much more exciting if you have helped to make some of those meals, instead of always eating food that others have made for you. Have you ever cooked a meal for anyone? When you do, you will see just how happy it makes people feel and how grateful they are for the time and care you have taken. This will make you feel proud too. It feels good when you cook for others.

the skills

Learning to cook is a bit like learning to read. When you learn to read, you learn the letters first and then you start to put the letters together to form words. It is similar to this when you learn to cook. You first learn some basic skills that you can later put together to make meals.

Cooking is not just about making something to eat; you will be practising maths (measuring, weighing, sharing), literacy (reading and writing if you jot down some notes about the recipes), geography (learning about food and where it comes from) and much more.

Cooking uses all your senses. You can look at food, smell it, touch it, taste it and listen to it as it cooks. This is something my mum taught me when I was young. I think that's pretty exciting; I hope you do, too.

the recipes

This book has 3 main chapters – Stage 1 (3–5 years), Stage 2 (5–7 years) and Stage 3 (7–11 years). Even though the recipes in Stage 1 are suitable for children aged 3–5 years, if you are older than that and have just picked this book up you can still make the recipes from this section. The recipes in Stage 1 are great for mixing and matching with the other recipes in the book to make a complete meal. For example, crunchy paprika chicken (page 28) is great after pretty prawn/shrimp cocktails (page 58) for a special supper, or three fruit salad (page 44) is a lovely dessert to have after pizzas (page 88).

All the recipes have been tested by children. I have included classic favourites like crumble topping (page 76), pastry (page 112), white sauce (page 96) and pizza dough (page 88). This is because I think that these are the basic building blocks for learning to cook. I was fortunate to be taught these recipes by my mother, my grandmother and my design technology teacher.

There are also lots of other exciting recipes in the book which use some ingredients that we are lucky to find at the store today. You can have a go at making your own sushi (page 102), you can see how to use corn tortillas (page 106) and you can have fun adding herbs and flowers to water to make your own ice bowl (page 70).

Remember that food is expensive, so don't be too disappointed if your parents don't want you to cook every day of the week. But the more you offer to make food that you can all eat as a family, the more likely it is that you will be able to cook, as your parents can include your food in their weekly budget.

Meat-free meals are good for both you and the planet – where possible, why not try to swap meat, fish or chicken for veggie or meat-free alternatives?

the photos

The children in the pictures are my friends' little ones, and they made the food you see in the photos with me.

your notes

As you work your way through a recipe, try to think about it: did you like cooking it and would you like to cook it again? You might like to write some notes in the book. I know that normally you are told not to write in books, but this one is for you to keep forever and you might find it handy to jot down a few comments to remind you of something for next time. For example, would you add more herbs or spice to a recipe? Or make double the amount so that you have enough for friends to share, too?

why we need to eat

The main reason why we need to eat good food is because it helps us to grow, develop and stay healthy. Ideally we need to eat 3 meals a day, with 2 small snacks in between. We also need to run around and play sport as much as possible, too, to help keep us fit and healthy.

There are certain types and amounts of food that we need to eat every day. We can eat everything, but we need to eat more of some foods than others. There are 5 main food groups:

1 Bread, rice, potatoes, pasta and other starchy foods

2 Fruit and vegetables

3 Milk and dairy foods

4 Meat, fish, eggs, beans and other non-dairy sources of protein

5 Foods and drinks that are high in fat and or sugar

Each day, ideally, we need to eat the following food:

• Each meal or snack should contain a food from the bread, cereals and potatoes section. This means that we eat these foods 5 times a day.

1 portion = a bowl of breakfast cereal or 2 tablespoons of pasta or rice.

• Each meal or snack should also contain a fruit or vegetable. We need 5 portions of fresh fruits and vegetables a day.

1 portion = 1 glass of fresh fruit juice, 1 piece of fruit, 2 tablespoons cooked vegetables.

• 3 portions of milk and dairy foods.

1 portion = 1 small glass of milk, 1 pot of yogurt, 1 tablespoon grated cheese.

• 1 or 2 portions of meat, fish and alternatives a day.

1 portion = 2 pink fish fingers (page 60) or an oven-baked herby burger (page 64).

We don't need to eat foods from the fatty and sugary food section every day, as fats and sugars are often found in foods in the other food groups above, but we can have them as treats. Homemade cakes and cookies are good for putting into packed lunches.

Did you know that all the food we eat comes from plants or animals? If possible, try to visit a local farm to see where animals are looked after and where crops are grown.

before you start cooking

Always ask an adult before you start to make sure that they are happy you are cooking and to check that they will be around to help if you need it.

Try to find all the ingredients and the equipment that you will need for the recipe before you start. Oven mitts are especially important!

You might like to wear an apron. This can help keep the dirt from your clothes falling into the food and also stop the food that you cook going all over your clothes.

Wash your hands before you begin and dry them on a clean towel.

Always try to help clear up after you have made something, and help others with the washing up and drying or loading the dishwasher. Your parents are far more likely to let you cook if you don't leave a huge mess behind.

This book is the beginning of your adventure with food and cooking!

Stage 1: **3-5 years**

grown-ups: this page is for you

children: you can skip this bit and have fun cooking!

I am sure you already know this, but I can't stress enough how cooking with children at this stage can have a positive benefit on their development in so many areas. As much as possible, try to let your child complete each step of the recipe on her own to help her to gain a sense of independence in the kitchen.

• Cooking will help your child with his physical development, for example his fine motor skills as well as his coordination of movement and eye-hand coordination. Just think about the range of physical skills that he needs to use scissors for cutting fresh herbs, to scoop flour from a container or bag or to brush melted butter onto dough.

• She can measure with spoons and is likely to be able to learn to count. This is why all the ingredients in this section need to be counted or measured with spoons (except for the chocolate kisses).

• He will start to work out how to share food evenly, e.g. dividing the fruit between the pies (page 42).

• She will start to understand the concept of time, e.g. how long things take to set or cook.

• Encouraging your child to cook at this stage can be helpful, as he can make a snack (page 26) or dinner for the family (page 28). He will become more confident with the recipes the more he makes them.

• Her attention span will be increasing and she will be able to choose to stop an activity and then come back to it again later.

• He will begin to sort things into simple categories, become interested in what causes things to happen and often ask 'why?'

• She will begin to be able to understand the concept of 'lots' or 'a little'; and she will be able to start to recognize primary colours.

• He will be able to help find the ingredients or equipment in the kitchen and match them to the pictures in the book.

• At this age, children love repetition. She will want to try the new skills over and over again.

• He is likely to be starting to enjoy the social element of sitting, talking and eating the food he has made with the rest of the family, and she can start to help with jobs like washing vegetables, and setting and clearing the table.

skills

You might find these skills useful for other things that you do (not just cooking), like watering the plants.

using an oven

Have you ever turned an oven on? Look at the recipe to see what temperature the oven needs to be at and then ask an adult to show you how to set the oven to that temperature. Most ovens have a little light that will go off when the oven has reached the right temperature. Always use oven mitts when you are putting food in or taking food out of the oven.

using a spoon to scoop

For example, you could try scooping some flour from a big bowl into a little bowl.

stirring & mixing

Try mixing ingredients together with different spoons, for example in the red dip on page 20.

counting

Practise counting the number of spoonfuls or ingredients that you need.

sorting

Look at the introduction on page 11 of the book to see the different categories of food. You could try sorting basic foods into each category.

spreading

Use a table knife to spread something soft like honey or butter onto toast. You will need to gently press the knife onto the food as you spread. Look at pages 26 and 27 for more spreading ideas.

pouring

Use small jugs/pitchers that are not too heavy, for pouring liquids from one container to another.

cutting with a table knife

A table knife is the knife you use to eat your meal with. It is not sharp. Practise cutting something soft like butter or avocado with a table knife.

opening & closing jars

Try opening the lid on a jar. Some jars will be very stiff and you will need some help opening them.

dipping

Sometimes you will need to coat a food in a crisp coating to protect the food when it is being cooked and to give it a lovely, crisp texture.

carry without spilling

Practise carrying liquids in containers without spilling them. The first time my son carried his fruit juice popsicles to the freezer with me when he was three years old we lost half the juice on the way to the freezer, but now we hardly ever have any spillages!

washing fruits & vegetables

Wash them in a bowl of water or put some water into the sink. It is a good idea to give salad vegetables and root vegetables, like carrots and potatoes that grow underneath the ground, a wash before they are eaten to remove the soil.

draining in a colander

A colander is like a bowl which has holes in it. It is useful for draining food like vegetables after you have washed them.

measuring with spoons

The recipes will either say 'tablespoon', which is a big spoon, or 'teaspoon', which is a small spoon. Make sure that you use the right spoon when you are measuring your ingredients.

sharing

In some recipes you will need to make sure that you share the food evenly, like sharing the fillings between tarts. You don't want all of the filling in some of the tarts and none in the others!

freezing

Freezers help to keep food fresh for a long time without it going bad. How does food freeze? Most food contains lots of water. Freezing works by changing this water to ice. Put a liquid into a freezer and watch it change to a solid. The solid is called ice. See page 39 for fruit juice popsicles.

touching food

When you touch food, think about how it feels – is it cold, slimy, hard or soft? Just remember never to lick your fingers after you have touched raw meat or fish.

mashing

This is when you squash food using a potato masher, fork or mortar and pestle. Practise with soft fruits, e.g. page 36, or garlic, e.g. page 18.

tearing

Try tearing some fresh herbs or lettuce leaves and then smelling them. My children used to like to smell mint, as they thought it smelled like toothpaste!

hulling strawberries

Use your fingers to pull the green stalks off the top of strawberries. You might need to dig your fingers into the fruit slightly to pull out the hard bit where the fruit and the stalk meet.

using biscuit /cookie cutters

Press the cutter into bread or pastry and twist it slightly to make sure that it cuts all the way through, and then lift the cutter up.

bashing with a pestle

You don't have to have one of these, but if you do, try bashing a peeled clove of garlic to make the salad dressing on page 18.

brushing

Use a pastry brush to brush milk, melted butter or oil. For example, brushing oil onto baking trays helps to stop the food from sticking to the trays.

rolling

Use a rolling pin to flatten something like bread (see page 22) or pastry (see page 42). When you roll pastry, try to roll small pieces of pastry, one at a time; it is much easier than rolling one big piece. Push the rolling pin down onto the pastry and roll it away from you.

Scooping out an avocado stone

Mixing eggs with a fork

Using a mortar and pestle

shaping

Use your hands to mould the food into a shape. For example, for the strawberry sweets/candies (page 38), you will need to mould the dough to make strawberry shapes. For the chocolate kisses (page 46), you need to mould the dough into small balls.

cutting with scissors

Always make sure that your fingers stay away from the scissors so that you don't cut them accidentally.

crushing garlic

Garlic grows in a 'bulb' with lots of small 'cloves' inside. Before you crush a clove of garlic you will need to peel it to remove the papery skin. Dig a fingernail into the skin to break it, then pull the skin away. To crush the clove put it in a garlic press and squeeze the press to close. You may need to scrape the crushed garlic off the press with a table knife. If you don't have a press, just bash the garlic with a rolling pin to release some of its juices and flavour and keep it whole.

setting the table

Have fun setting the table and clearing away. The fork sits on the left of the plate and the knife on the right. The knife blade faces towards the plate.

tasting new foods

Try something new – you might like it. You will also need to taste the food that you have made to check that it tastes good before other people try it. Use a teaspoon to taste your food.

kitchen equipment

These are a few things that you might find useful to have in the kitchen, however you don't need them all to do some cooking.

oven

There are so many different types of ovens. Ask your parents to show you how yours works. Most ovens have a little light on them which will go off when the oven has reached the right temperature.

oven mitts

You can't cook safely without these. Whenever you help to put anything in or take anything out of the oven you must always put your oven mitts on! It is very easy to burn yourself.

scissors

If you don't have kitchen scissors, use paper scissors to snip herbs but make sure that you wash them before and after you use them to cut up food. When you use scissors, always keep your fingers away from the blades so that you don't accidentally cut yourself.

measuring spoons

You will need 2 different sizes of spoon for recipes: a 'tablespoon', which is a big spoon and a 'teaspoon', which is a small spoon. Make sure that you use the right spoon when you are measuring your ingredients.

rolling pin

These come in all different sizes, they are easy to use and great fun. They are needed for rolling out dough or bread and they can be used for bashing olives to help remove their stones and bashing garlic cloves to help remove their skins!

cutters

These come in all different shapes and sizes. Have fun cutting out circles of bread for the tasty bread tarts (page 34).

sieve/strainer

Why do we need to use a sieve/strainer? To remove any lumps and to add air so that the food we cook is light.

mixing spoons

Wooden and melamine spoons are both great for mixing ingredients together.

pastry brush

This is useful for brushing melted butter onto pastry, like the mini fruit pies on page 42 or for brushing oil onto baking trays, e.g. the burgers on page 64 (if you are not using parchment paper).

pestle & mortar

You don't need one of these but they are fun to use for bashing food like cloves of garlic to make a dressing for a salad like on page 18. If you don't have one you can use a small rolling pin and a little bowl instead. The pestle is the stick and the mortar is the name given to the bowl.

potato masher or fork

This is for mashing soft fruit and vegetables.

melon baller

If you don't have one of these, you can use a small teaspoon instead.

garlic press

Peel the garlic clove first and then put the clove inside the garlic press. Push down to squeeze the garlic out (see page 15).

cutting board

Always wash your cutting board after you have used it. This is very important if you have cut meat, poultry or fish on it.

muffin tin/pan

You need this for the bread tarts on page 34 and you can also use it to make small cakes.

baking tray/sheet

These are very handy. For example, you will need one for the DIY pizzas on page 32, and many other things which you cook in the oven.

mixing bowl

These come in all different shapes and sizes. They are useful for so many different recipes, whether you are making a cake or mixing leaves together to make a salad.

colander

This is like a sieve/strainer but it has bigger holes. It is great for draining things like cooked pasta or a jar of olives.

wire cooling rack

You don't have to have one of these, but it is useful for helping food to cool down.

measuring jugs/cups

Available in different sizes, use these for measuring liquids. The spout makes it easy to carefully pour a liquid.

fork, table knife, spoon

This is the cutlery that you use to eat with.

big & small bowl, plate

Hopefully these will not be too difficult to find in your kitchen cupboards.

Flattening dough with a rolling pin

Using a melon baller

Buttering a baking tray

salad bar with a delicious dressing

This is a recipe for a salad dressing. It is very useful to know how to make a good dressing so that you can always enjoy eating yummy salads. It is my children's idea to make a 'salad bar'. They like to choose salad ingredients from the fridge, put them into bowls and then we all help ourselves. Sometimes they choose things like grated carrot, tinned sweetcorn/corn kernels and crunchy bread croutons to go with the salad greens.

SKILLS

using mortar & pestle
measuring with spoons
cutting with table knife
mixing • washing • pouring

INGREDIENTS

For 4 people you need:

DRESSING

1 garlic clove

tiny pinch of salt (see Tips opposite)

1 teaspoon mustard (English, whole-grain or Dijon are all fine)

1 teaspoon balsamic vinegar

1 tablespoon white wine vinegar

a little freshly ground black pepper

6 tablespoons olive oil

SALAD INGREDIENTS

You can use any salad ingredients that you like. Here are some that we often use:

ripe avocado (see Tips opposite) and cooked, peeled fresh beetroot/beets (you can chop these using a table knife)

salad greens e.g. lettuce leaves, rocket/arugula, watercress, baby spinach leaves

cherry tomatoes, pitted olives, pine nuts, small mozzarella balls

mortar and pestle • table knife cutting board • several small bowls colander • clean kitchen towel small jug/pitcher

1 To make the dressing, peel the thin, pink skin away from the garlic clove and if you have a mortar and pestle, put the garlic into the bowl, add a tiny pinch of salt (see Tips opposite) and bash the garlic until you have a paste. If you don't have a mortar and pestle, crush the garlic in a garlic press and put into a small jug/pitcher, then use a small whisk to whisk everything together.

2 Add the mustard, balsamic vinegar and white wine vinegar and a little freshly ground black pepper and mix again.

TIPS

• Please ask an adult or older child to cut the avocado in half.

• I don't add salt to any recipes for children, but this is an exception, as the salt helps you to mash the garlic to a paste.

3 Add the olive oil a little at a time – keep mixing all the time so that you end up with a smooth dressing. This will come with practice. Keep making it every time you have a salad!

4 If you have some soft foods, like avocado (see Tips above) or beetroot/beets, you might like to cut these into small pieces using a table knife and then put them into bowls.

5 Wash the lettuce in a colander in the sink, then shake or dry with a clean kitchen towel. Put the lettuce in a bowl and then put all your other salad ingredients into small bowls. Pour your dressing into a small jug/pitcher. Let everyone help themselves to the pick 'n' mix salad bar. You will have some salad dressing left over to use another day. Keep it in a clean jar in the fridge.

red dip with crunchy veggies

Parents seem to like this dip just as much as the children do and it's a great way to try different vegetables, too. You could also make some tortilla chips from page 30 to eat with the dip.

INGREDIENTS

For 2–3 people you need:

2 tablespoons tomato ketchup

4 tablespoons cream cheese

2 handfuls each: sugar snap peas, baby corn, small carrots and cherry tomatoes

spoon • mixing bowl • bowl of water clean kitchen towel • small bowl • plate

SKILLS

washing vegetables • using spoon counting • mixing • dipping

1 Count the spoons of tomato ketchup into a mixing bowl and then spoon the cream cheese into the bowl. You might need a small spoon to scrape the cream cheese from the big spoon. Mix to make an orangey-red mixture.

2 Wash the vegetables – put them in a bowl of water and wipe with your hands to get rid of any dirt or grit. If you clean the carrots really well, you won't need to peel them. Gently shake the vegetables to dry them or spread them on a clean kitchen towel to dry out.

3 Spoon the red dip into a small bowl and put it on a plate. Count the dry vegetables as you place them on the plate next to the dip. Now dip the vegetables into the dip and enjoy eating!

roly-poly sandwich

You can use any fillings you like in this sandwich – here we've used smoked salmon but thinly-sliced beetroot would work well too. Try different types of bread like wholemeal/whole-wheat, white or multigrain. Have a look in your local bakery or supermarket at all the different kinds. If you have had fun making these sandwiches, you might like to try the Super Sushi Rolls on page 102, which are also rolled into pretty spiral shapes.

INGREDIENTS

For 1 roly-poly sandwich you need:

1 slice wholemeal/whole-wheat, white or multigrain bread

1 tablespoon cream cheese

2 slices smoked salmon or thinly sliced beetroot

a little mustard and cress

table knife • rolling pin • small plate

SKILLS

spreading • rolling • cutting with table knife

1 Put the slice of bread on a clean surface and use a table knife to cut the crusts off.

2 Flatten the slice of bread by rolling over it with a rolling pin.

3 Spread the cream cheese onto the bread with the table knife.

4 Lay the smoked salmon on top of the cream cheese and then sprinkle the mustard and cress over the salmon.

5 Starting with a short side of the bread slice, roll the bread up into a long sausage shape.

6 Cut the sausage shape with the table knife into 5 roly-poly sandwiches. When you lay them flat on a plate you'll see that you have made spirals!

OTHER FILLING IDEAS

• A little canned salmon or tuna, drained and mashed with a fork, mixed with a little mayonnaise, then scattered with a few torn lettuce or spinach leaves over the top.

• Grated cheese, ham torn into very small pieces and a finely chopped tomato.

cheesy stuffed peppers

You need to choose small sweet (bell) peppers from a greengrocer or a large supermarket for this recipe. These cheesy stuffed peppers are easy to make and eat and are great with some crusty bread for a packed lunch or a quick snack. Don't forget to smell the herbs when you are choosing which ones to add to your cream cheese mixture.

INGREDIENTS

For 1 mini pepper you need:

1 mini sweet (bell) pepper, top cut off (please ask an adult or older child to do this)

about 1 tablespoon cream cheese

2 teaspoons plain yogurt

a few fresh herb leaves e.g. dill, thyme, sage or parsley

mixing bowl • spoon • scissors

SKILLS

mixing • spooning • smelling herbs

1 Use your fingers to scrape the little seeds out of the mini (bell) pepper.

2 Put the cream cheese and yogurt in a mixing bowl and mix together with a spoon.

3 Pick the leaves off some herbs, or using scissors, snip the herb leaves into small pieces and add to the cream cheese mixture. Stir with the spoon. Spoon the cheese mixture into the pepper and put the lid back on top.

ants on a log

This is a quick and easy snack that you can make all by yourself. It's also a good way to practise spreading, which will be useful when you make your own sandwiches and put jam or honey on your toast for breakfast.

INGREDIENTS

For 2 celery boats you need:

1 celery stick/rib, cut in half

a little peanut butter

10 dried cranberries, raisins or other dried fruit

bowl of water • clean kitchen towel table knife

SKILLS

washing vegetables • spreading • counting

1 Wash the celery – put it in a bowl of water and wipe with your hands to get rid of any dirt or grit. Gently shake the celery to dry it or dry it with a clean kitchen towel.

2 Use a table knife to spread some peanut butter into the celery stick pieces.

3 Count 5 dried fruits and stick them onto the peanut butter.

cucumber snacks

For an extra-quick snack you could try spreading some cream cheese onto cucumber slices and decorating them with pieces of dried apricot to make them look a bit like buttons. They taste yummy too!

INGREDIENTS

For 4 buttons you need:

4 slices cucumber

1 tablespoon cream cheese

1 dried apricot

table knife • scissors

SKILLS

spreading • counting • using scissors

1 Use a table knife to spread a little cream cheese on top of each cucumber slice.

2 Using scissors, snip the dried apricots into small pieces.

3 Dot the apricot pieces over the cream cheese, counting them as you go: how many pieces have you added?

crunchy paprika bites

These are just as delicious if you make them with cauliflower instead of chicken. Try different coatings, such as crunchy biscuits/crackers for cheese or breadcrumbs; you can even try cornflakes.

 SKILLS

crushing • counting • dipping • using oven

INGREDIENTS

For 4 people you need:

about 10 dry biscuits for cheese/whole-grain crackers (or 10 tablespoons cornflakes)

1 large pinch paprika

4 tablespoons tomato purée/paste (or ketchup)

4 free-range skinless chicken thigh fillets, cut into pieces (about 425 g/14 oz.) or small cauliflower florets

salad and boiled new potatoes go well with the chicken

*scissors • parchment paper
2 baking trays • 2 mixing bowls
spoon • oven mitts*

1 Turn the oven on to 180°C (350°F) Gas 4. Cut 2 pieces of parchment paper, each big enough to cover the baking trays, or brush a little olive oil over the trays. Count the biscuits/crackers into a mixing bowl and use your fingers to crush them into very small pieces. Add the paprika to the bowl, too, and mix with your hands.

2 Count the 4 spoonfuls of tomato purée/paste into another bowl.

3 Dip the chicken pieces or cauliflower into the tomato so that there is a bit all over every piece.

WASH YOUR HANDS

You must always wash your hands thoroughly after handling raw meat.

4 Dip the pieces of chicken or cauliflower into the crushed biscuits/crackers so that they stick to the chicken.

5 Put the crunchy chicken or cauliflower straight onto the lined baking trays. Now, WASH YOUR HANDS (see above).

6 Ask an adult to help you put the trays into the oven using oven mitts. Cook for 20 minutes or until the pieces are golden brown and cooked all the way through – ask an adult to help you check this.

green dip with tortilla chips

When you have friends around, you could have this as an appetizer. It's a great way to use up corn tortillas that might be past their best. You can also make these with pita bread.

INGREDIENTS

For 4 people you need:

4 corn tortillas

1 garlic clove

handful fresh coriander/cilantro leaves

½ lime

2 ripe avocados, cut in half (ask an adult or older child to cut the avocados in half)

scissors • baking tray • oven mitts
mortar & pestle • spoon • small bowl

SKILLS

using scissors • using mortar & pestle • using teaspoon • mashing

1 Turn the oven on to 180°C (350°F) Gas 4. Using scissors, snip the corn tortillas into small pieces and put on a baking tray. Ask an adult to help you put the tray into the oven using oven mitts. Bake for 5 minutes until golden and starting to crisp. Ask an adult to help you take the chips out of the oven.

2 Peel the garlic (see page 88 for help). If you have a mortar and pestle, put the garlic into the mortar (bowl) and bash with the pestle until you have a paste. If you don't have a mortar and pestle, use the end of a small rolling pin and a bowl. Using scissors, snip the coriander/cilantro into small pieces.

3 Add the coriander/cilantro to the mortar. Squeeze the juice from the lime half into the mortar. Mash with the pestle.

4 Scoop the stones out of the avocados with a teaspoon and peel away the skins.

5 Add some of the avocado flesh to the mortar and mash. Add the rest of the avocado flesh and mash again until you have a lumpy paste. Spoon the dip into a small bowl and serve with the corn chips.

DIY pizzas

Making pizzas with flour tortillas, English muffins, pita bread, or French bread is quick and you can use any topping ingredients you have in your kitchen. You can even cook these on a campfire – roll the tortilla up into a sausage shape first, wrap in foil and ask an adult to put it on the fire for 10 minutes.

INGREDIENTS

To make 4 pizzas you need:

4 flour tortillas, pieces French bread, halved English muffins or rolls

6 teaspoons canned tomato passata/purée or chopped tomatoes for each pizza

your choice of toppings:
grated cheese, canned tuna, pitted olives, sweetcorn/corn kernels, pieces ham or salami, sliced (bell) pepper, sliced mushrooms, sliced cherry tomatoes

scissors • parchment paper
2 baking trays • spoon • oven mitts
cutting board • table knife

SKILLS

spreading • choosing toppings
cutting with table knife • using oven

1 Turn the oven on to 200°C (400°F) Gas 6. Cut 2 pieces of parchment paper, each big enough to cover the baking trays. Put 2 tortillas on each baking tray.

2 Count 6 teaspoons of tomato passata/purée onto each tortilla.

3 Use the back of the spoon to spread the tomato over the tortillas but leave a little border around the edge so that it doesn't drip over the edges when the pizza is in the oven.

4 Choose some toppings and sprinkle them over the tomato. Ask an adult to help you put the baking trays into the oven using oven mitts. Bake for 5 minutes.

5 Ask an adult to help you take the cooked pizzas out of the oven using oven mitts and put them onto a cutting board. Using a table knife, cut them in half, then in half again to make quarters.

tasty bread tarts

It can be frustrating if you want to cook something but you don't have the ingredients to do it. These tarts use basic ingredients that you should find in your kitchen like bread, milk and eggs. You can add other fillings like corn and tuna.

SKILLS

cutting shapes with cutters and sharing toppings between the cases • cracking eggs

INGREDIENTS

To make 6 tarts you need:

a little unsalted butter

6 slices brown/multigrain bread

3 free-range eggs and 4 tablespoons milk (or 2 eggs and 6 tablespoons milk)

handful fresh mint leaves (or other herbs) – have you ever smelt fresh mint leaves? They smell amazing!

2 handfuls frozen (and defrosted) or fresh peas or sweetcorn/corn kernels

small handful grated Parmesan

scrap of parchment paper • muffin tin/pan • round cutter as wide as the slices of bread • cutting board oven mitts • table knife • small jug/pitcher • spoon • fork • scissors

1 Turn the oven on to 190˚C (375˚F) Gas 5. Take the round cutter and press it into each slice of bread on a cutting board to cut out 6 circles.

2 Using a scrap of parchment paper, rub some butter inside 6 of the holes in the muffin tin/pan. Press each bread circle into the buttered muffin tin holes. Ask an adult to help you put the muffin tin into the oven using oven mitts. Bake for 5 minutes. Ask an adult to help you take the muffin tin out of the oven using oven mitts and let cool.

3 Now you need to crack open the eggs: hold an egg in one hand and carefully use a table knife to crack the egg in the middle. Put your thumbs into the crack and pull the egg shell apart. Let the egg fall into a small jug/pitcher. Repeat with the other eggs. (See page 60 for a photo of how to crack eggs.) Mix the eggs with a fork to break them up. Add the milk and mix the milk and eggs together with a fork again.

CRACKING EGGS

I have shown you how to crack eggs, which is in the next section of the book, but you might like to start practicing this skill now. don't worry if some shell falls in with the egg – just fish it out with a spoon.

4 Using scissors, snip the mint into small pieces and put a little into each tart. Now put a few peas into each tart too – try to share them out evenly so that the tarts have roughly the same amount.

5 Slowly pour the egg mixture that's in the jug/pitcher into the tarts over the peas and mint – try to stop pouring just before you reach the top, as the tarts will rise in the oven.

6 Sprinkle a little grated Parmesan over the tarts. Ask an adult to help you put the muffin tin back in the oven using oven mitts. Cook for 12 minutes, or until they have puffed up and the egg is cooked.

fizzy strawberry crush

This is great for practising mashing fruit and pouring from a measuring jug/cup. This drink is made with fizzy water, so you need to drink it straightaway before the bubbles disappear. If you don't like fizz, just add more fruit juice instead.

INGREDIENTS

To make 2 glasses you need:

2 large handfuls ripe strawberries

orange juice to half fill your glasses

fizzy water (or if you don't want fizz, add more juice or still water)

bowl • potato masher • spoon glass • measuring jug/cup • 2 glasses

SKILLS

hulling strawberries • mashing • spooning • pouring

1 Hull the strawberries – this means to pull the green stalks off the tops. You might need to dig your fingers into the strawberries to really pull the tops out.

2 Put the strawberries into a bowl and mash with a potato masher.

3 Spoon the strawberries into a jug/pitcher.

4 Pour the orange juice onto the strawberries and mix with a spoon.

5 Pour the fizzy water into the jug/pitcher and mix again with the spoon.

6 Pour the drink into 2 glasses. Drink right away! If you haven't had a fizzy drink before, you might find that the bubbles feel funny in your mouth.

strawberry candy

Even though these are quick to make, you will need to have some patience and wait for the sweets/candy to dry after you have made it. This is just like playing with play dough!

SKILLS

mashing • making dough • shaping using scissors

INGREDIENTS

To make about 20 strawberries you need:

1 ripe strawberry (eat some more fresh strawberries while you're waiting for the sweets to set!)

1 tablespoon cream cheese

½ capful vanilla extract

about 300 g/2 cups icing/confectioners' sugar (you may need slightly more or less)

long thin green sweets/candies to make strawberry 'stalks'

mixing bowl • fork • parchment paper plate • scissors • pretty serving plate

1 Hull the strawberry – this means to pull the green stalk off the top using your fingers. Put the strawberry, cream cheese and vanilla into a mixing bowl and mash with a fork.

2 Add 3 spoonfuls of the icing/confectioners' sugar to the bowl and mix again. Add 3 more spoonfuls and keep mixing. You might want to use your hands now to mix. Keep adding sugar until you have a firm dough that is not too sticky.

3 Take a small piece of the mixture – about the size of a real strawberry – and shape it into a ball. Now squash it into a strawberry shape and put onto a plate. (You might like to put a piece of parchment paper on the plate first so that the strawberries don't stick to the plate.) Take the fork and push it into the strawberries to make holes.

4 Using scissors, cut the green sweets/candies into short pieces, then cut a few slits into each piece so that they fan open to look like leaves. Push into the strawberries and let dry for 3–4 hours. Transfer them to a pretty plate before you serve them!

stripey fruit juice pops

This is a great way to learn about freezing and watching liquid change to a solid. You can use yogurt tubs or plastic cups, and wooden lolly/popsicle sticks or plastic spoons. Don't use metal spoons as they will be too cold to hold when they freeze.

INGREDIENTS

To make as many as you like, you need:

purple fruit juice (I used blackcurrant but you could also try a red fruit juice like raspberry)

cloudy apple juice

old yogurt tubs, plastic cups or lolly moulds • spoons or sticks • you will also need to make sure there is room in your freezer to stand all your yogurt tubs or lolly moulds upright

SKILLS
pouring (juice into moulds) • freezing (changing texture)

1 Find some old yogurt tubs and make sure that they are clean and dry. You will also need some wooden lolly/popsicle sticks or plastic spoons – you should have enough of these to go in all your yogurt tubs. Put one stick or spoon into each yogurt tub. Start pouring the purple fruit juice into a yogurt tub until it's half full. Repeat this with all your other yogurt tubs. You might like to pour the purple juice first into some of the tubs and the apple juice first into the other tubs so that the stripes look different when the pops are frozen.

2 Put the tubs into the freezer and freeze until frozen – this will take at least 4 hours. Take the tubs out of the freezer and pour the other juice over the frozen juice until you nearly reach the top of the tub. Don't fill them too full!

3 Put the tubs back into the freezer and freeze again for 4 hours or until you have frozen ice popsicles. When you take the popsicles out of the freezer, you might need to sit each one in a little warm water to help ease the popsicle itself out of the tub, but don't let it sit in the warm water for long otherwise it will melt.

berry crunch

This is like a very thick fruit smoothie but with some crunch added. It makes a wonderful breakfast, dessert or snack. The amounts in this recipe are only a guide, as the exact quantities will vary depending on the size of glasses that you decide to use.

INGREDIENTS

For 2 glasses you need:

4 handfuls fresh berries

4 tablespoons plain Greek yogurt

8 tablespoons crunchy cereal or muesli

bowl • fork • spoon • 2 glasses

SKILLS

mashing • spooning • mixing

1 Put most of the berries into a bowl (save a few for decorating the top) and mash with a fork or potato masher.

2 Count the spoons of yogurt into the bowl with the mashed berries and mix with the spoon.

3 Spoon a bit of the cereal into the bottom of the glasses and spoon the fruity yogurt on top of the cereal. You will start to see layers in the glasses. Spoon a little more cereal on top of the yogurt and then dollop some more yogurt on top of the cereal. Finish with the saved berries on top.

mini fruit pies

Ready-made puff pastry dough is just right for these mini fruit pies. When you are rolling pastry, it is much easier to roll one small piece at a time instead of rolling one large piece, which is why I have broken the pastry into 4 pieces. These pastries taste delicious and are good for packed lunches, at snack time or for desserts. If you choose to use big dried fruits like mango or apricots, you will need to use scissors to cut them into small pieces first.

SKILLS

mixing • rolling pastry • cutting circles • brushing • using oven

INGREDIENTS

To make 16 mini pies you need:

small piece of butter, about the size of 2 pieces of chocolate, melted (ask an adult or older child to do this), plus a little extra

20 tablespoons (200 g/1⅓ cups) dried fruits

1 teaspoon mixed spice

375 g/12½ oz. puff pastry dough

a little flour for sprinkling

a little demerara sugar for sprinkling

scissors • parchment paper • spoon baking tray • mixing bowl • rolling pin pound coin or 2 pennies • round cutter about 6 cm/2¼ inches across table knife • pastry brush

1 Turn the oven on to 180°C (350°F) Gas 4. Cut a piece of parchment paper big enough to cover the baking tray. Put the melted butter, dried fruits and spice in a mixing bowl and mix with a spoon.

2 Break the dough in half, then break each piece in half to make 4 pieces. Sprinkle a little flour on the work surface. Flatten one piece of dough with a rolling pin until it is about the same thickness as a pound coin or 2 stacked pennies.

3 Take the cutter and, starting at the edge of the dough, push it down to cut out circles. Keep going until you have used up all of that dough. Roll out another piece of dough and cut out circles. Repeat with the rest of the dough. Using a teaspoon, spoon a little fruit mixture onto the middle of each circle. Bring the edges of the circle up together to seal the mixture inside. There should be no gaps in the pastry!

4 Turn the parcels over and flatten slightly with your hand. Using a table knife, carefully cut 2 or 3 short slits in the top of each pastry – this will let the steam escape when the pastries are baking.

5 Put them on the baking tray. Dip a pastry brush in a little melted butter and brush over all the pies. Sprinkle with sugar. Ask an adult to help you put the tray in the oven and bake for 15 minutes. They should look golden!

three fruit salad

Have you ever made melon balls before? It's great fun scooping the melon flesh into balls. A melon baller doesn't cost very much to buy – just look in any good kitchen store. If you don't have a melon baller, you can use a small teaspoon. You can make a fruit salad with other fruits as well, like strawberries, raspberries and sliced peaches. It's tasty, colourful and good for you, too!

INGREDIENTS

For 3 people you need:

½ ripe melon (seeds removed)

2 satsumas/tangerines

1 ripe banana

150 ml/⅔ cup orange and mango juice (or other juice of your choice)

melon baller or small rounded teaspoon pretty bowl • table knife • spoon

SKILLS

using melon baller • pouring

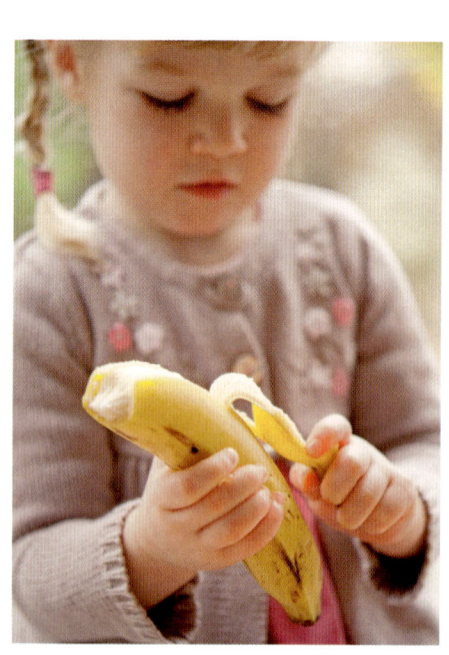

1 Use a melon baller or a teaspoon to scoop out small balls of melon flesh and put into a pretty bowl for the fruit salad.

2 Peel the satsumas/tangerines and then, using a table knife, cut each segment in half. Add to the bowl of melon balls.

3 Peel the banana.

4 Using the table knife again, cut the banana into small pieces. Add to the bowl.

5 Pour the juice over the fruit and stir together.

chocolate kisses

This is the first recipe in the book that needs the ingredients to be weighed. There is more information about weighing in Stage 2 of the book. If you weigh everything before you start cooking, the rest is very easy.

SKILLS

buttering baking trays • shaping • mashing creaming butter and sugar (see page 51)

INGREDIENTS

To make 25 kisses you need:

200 g/1 stick plus 5 tablespoons unsalted butter, soft

100 g/½ cup golden caster or granulated sugar

capful vanilla extract

250 g/2 cups self-raising/rising flour

2 tablespoons cocoa powder

RASPBERRY CREAM

4 ripe raspberries

100 g/6½ tablespoons unsalted butter, soft

100 g/⅔ cup icing/confectioners' sugar

scrap of paper • 2 baking trays mixing bowl • wooden spoon oven mitts • small bowl • fork

1 Turn the oven on to 180˚C (350˚F) Gas 4. Take a scrap of paper and use it to rub a little butter over 2 baking trays.

2 Put the soft butter, sugar and vanilla extract in a mixing bowl and mix well with a wooden spoon until it becomes fluffy and paler in colour. This helps to beat air into the mixture.

3 Tip the flour and cocoa powder into the bowl and mix well with your hands.

4 Break the mixture into 5. Now break each piece into 10 pieces, all the same size. Roll each piece into a small ball the size of a small walnut, then flatten a bit. Put onto the baking trays and ask an adult to help you put them in the oven using oven mitts. Bake for 6–7 minutes, then ask an adult to help you take the trays out of the oven. Let cool.

5 For the raspberry cream, put the berries into a small bowl, mash with a fork, then add the butter and sugar and mix with the fork.

6 Spoon a little cream onto a kiss and sandwich with another kiss. Keep going until you have 25 kisses.

Stage 2: 5-7 years

grown-ups: this page is for you

children: you can skip this bit and have fun cooking!

As your child works through these recipes, help him to link them up with recipes and skills from the previous chapter. He could make the red dip as a starter (page 20), then the oven-baked herby burgers from this chapter for the main course.

• At some point during this stage, she is likely to be ready to learn how to use a small, sharp knife for cutting, but make sure that you always stay with her and guide her to follow safe cutting techniques.

• Your child will be more aware of size, shape and weight. Encourage him to guess the weights of random objects and then weigh them to see what the result is. Also encourage him to measure all the ingredients for a recipe before he starts cooking.

• She will be growing towards reading and writing independently. Encourage her to read some of the words and to follow the sequence of steps for the recipes with the photos to guide her.

• He will be more willing to work out what he needs to do next, so try to avoid the temptation to tell him. As much as possible, let him work through recipes on his own.

• She will be more expressive with her language and more willing to share what she thinks of a recipe. After she has made something, ask her about it, e.g. if she would change anything if she made it again.

• He will start to show an interest in the science behind food and will enjoy watching food like couscous change from small, inedible hard pellets to something soft that is good to eat.

• She will be ready to use more complex kitchen equipment, like graters or lemon juicers.

• Encourage him to use his imagination by adding his own ingredients e.g. other toppings to the tomato tarts on page 56.

• She will be able to help work out how long the food needs to cook in the oven and how to share the food evenly between the whole family.

• He will have an increased interest in the world around him and where food comes from. Help him to understand that all the food we eat comes from plants and animals and that some of these plants grow in other countries.

• She will want to help with simple tasks like setting and clearing the table, and this will help with her social development.

skills

I hope that you enjoyed learning the skills in Stage 1. Here are some more to have fun practising as you cook some new recipes.

using a grill/broiler

Does your oven have a grill/broiler? Most ovens do. When you turn it on, the element will heat up until it is red. If you put some food underneath the grill/broiler, like the bagel on page 66, it will toast it until it is golden and bubbling. Always use oven mitts when you are putting food under or removing food from the grill/broiler.

knives

Always ask an adult before you use a sharp knife. It is likely that you will be ready now, with help from an adult, to use a small paring knife. The safest and most popular ways to use a knife are the bridge-cutting and claw-cutting techniques.

bridge-cutting technique

Hold the food between a thumb and finger of one hand to make a bridge. Hold a small paring knife in the other hand, put the blade under the bridge and cut downwards through the food.

claw-cutting technique

Make your fingers into a 'claw' shape, tucking your thumb inside your fingers. Use this claw to hold the food. Hold a small paring knife in your other hand and cut the food. As the knife moves along the food, pull the claw away from the knife.

grating

Hold the handle of the grater with one hand and then push the cheese downwards over the grater 'teeth'. Always keep your fingers away from the grater 'teeth', as they are very sharp.

lining a baking tin/pan

You will need to sit the tin/pan on the paper first and draw around it before you cut it with scissors. If you do this, the paper should fit inside the tin.

measuring

Have you ever measured a liquid before? Fill a jug/pitcher with water. You will then need a glass measuring jug/cup: this is a clear glass jug/pitcher with measurements written up the side. Carefully pour water into the measuring jug/cup, up to the level that you need e.g. 150 ml/½ cup.

Grating cheese

Cracking an egg

Cutting a lemon

measuring volume

If you want to work out the 'volume' of a container (that is how much liquid the container will hold), first fill it with water, then pour this water into a measuring jug/cup. Write down the level on the measuring jug/cup on a piece of paper. You then know how much liquid you need to fill the container. You could practise this by making some stripey frozen fruit popsicles (page 39).

weighing

Learn how to use weighing scales. All scales are different, so ask an adult to show you how to use yours. Why don't you try weighing some fruits or vegetables such as a banana or 2 apples. You could also see if you can guess how much you think something will weigh and then put it on the scales to see what the result is.

sharing & dividing

When you have made a large quantity of mixture, you may need to divide it up into small amounts before you cook it. For example, for the burgers on page 64, you need to divide the mixture into 8 equal pieces. To do this, first cut the mixture into 2 equal pieces (halves), then cut each half in half to make 4 equal pieces (quarters) and then cut each quarter in half again to make eighths.

shaping

Use your hands to help you shape any mixture.

how to crack an egg

There are 2 ways to crack eggs. Either hold an egg in one hand and carefully use a table knife to crack the egg in the middle. Put your thumbs into the crack and pull the egg shell apart. Let the egg fall into a jug/pitcher or bowl and mix with a fork. Fish out any egg shell with a spoon. Or, if you prefer, you can crack an egg by bashing it on the side of a bowl, but you might end up with some of the egg dripping down the side of the bowl until you've had a chance to practise! Always wash your hands well after cracking eggs, as it is very easy to pass bacteria from raw food like eggs to cooked food.

opening cans

This will take some practice and you need to be careful, as cans are sharp. Ask an adult to show you how to use your can opener, as they all differ.

melting chocolate & butter

Heat the chocolate and butter very, very gently in a saucepan over low heat so that the chocolate melts slowly.

rubbing butter into flour

Once you know how to rub fat into flour you can make pastry, crumble toppings or biscuits/cookies. Make sure the butter is really cold. Use a table knife to cut the cold butter into small pieces, add to the flour and gently rub the pieces of butter between the tips of your thumbs and fingers so they flatten and gradually mix into the flour. Keep lifting your fingertips above the bowl, as this will let air get to the flour and keep the mixture cool. Try not to use your whole hands, as this will melt the butter.

creaming butter & sugar

The most common way to make cakes and many biscuits/cookies is to begin by creaming softened butter with sugar – this means beating the sugar and butter together either with a wooden spoon or an electric mixer until the mixture is very pale and fluffy. This adds air to the mixture and gives it a light and fluffy, almost mousse-like texture. Before you begin: use unsalted butter (it has a better flavour than margarine) and you will need to take it out of the fridge some time before you start so that it is soft. If the butter is too hard you will not be able to beat in a lot of air and the cake may not rise as well.

folding

This is when you carefully mix a cake mixture, almost cutting it with the spoon to 'fold' it rather than mix it. This method adds air to the mixture so that it stays light and airy. It is easier if you use a metal spoon instead of a wooden spoon.

breadcrumbing

Dip the food into a little beaten egg, then dip into breadcrumbs and turn to coat the food evenly.

marinating

A marinade can actually start to soften food and break it down, so do you need to be careful how long you let the food sit in marinade. For example, fish left to marinate in lemon juice and oil will start to cook as it sits in the lemon juice.

kitchen equipment

There's lots more to explore in the kitchen now that you are getting used to cooking and using different types of equipment. Here are a few that might be good to try.

weighing scales

The great thing with cooking is that you can practise things you are learning at school, like maths, when you measure and weigh out ingredients. Ask your parents if they have a set of scales that you can use. There are lots of different types, so ask an adult to show you how to use them.

garlic press

This is easy and good fun to use. Make sure that you peel the pink skin away from the garlic clove before you crush it.

grater

Remember that the small 'teeth' can be as sharp as little knives, so make sure that you always keep your fingers away from them. Graters come in different shapes and sizes and the 'teeth' on the graters vary in size.

palette knife

This is handy for lifting things.

measuring jug/cups

You will need a glass measuring jug/cup for liquids. US readers will need a set of measuring cups for dry ingredients.

saucepans

Ideally you need a small saucepan for pasta sauces and a large pan for cooking pasta (see page 94).

small, sharp knife

A small paring knife is the best knife to begin with. Once you know how to hold your knife and cut food safely, there are so many things that you can make to eat. The main cutting techniques are the 'bridge' and the 'claw' (see page 50). Once you have learned these, you can cut most things safely, but always ask an adult before you use a sharp knife.

spatula

This is ideal for scraping a bowl clean, but you might prefer to use your fingers (if the mixture is safe to eat – check with an adult)!

can opener

Some foods come in cans and some cans have a ring pull, which makes them easy to open. Others will require a can opener. Let an adult help you the first time you use one.

lemon juicer

If you don't have a juicer, cut the fruit into smaller pieces and squeeze the juice out by hand. You will probably need to strain the juice to ensure that you remove any seeds.

baking tins/pans

Loaf tins/pans, small round tins or square tins are all used to bake cakes.

round cutter

This is helpful for cutting out biscuits/ cookies or small tarts like on page 56 but if you don't have a cutter, you can use a small cup or bowl instead. Cutters can come in fun shapes, too.

ovenproof dish

You will need a dish that won't crack when you put it into the oven for recipes like the what's-in-season fruit crumble on page 76. These come in different shapes, sizes and colours and you will probably have a couple in your kitchen cupboard.

Grater

Weighing scales

Saucepan

Round cutters

Ovenproof dish

Can opener

Measuring jug

Loaf tin/pan

Lemon juicer and sieve

herby scrambled eggs

Did you know that the yolk of the egg is orange and the clear part is called the white? Scrambled eggs are a great, simple recipe to learn, as once you know how to make them, you can make them for your lunch, breakfast or supper.

INGREDIENTS

For 1 person you need:

fresh herb e.g. parsley leaves or chives

2 free-range eggs

4 cherry tomatoes

a little unsalted butter

buttered toast, to eat with the eggs

scissors • mixing bowl • table knife spoon • fork • small paring knife saucepan • heatproof pan stand/trivet

SKILLS

cracking eggs • using saucepan • using knife

1 Using scissors, snip some herbs into small pieces and put in a mixing bowl. Now you need to crack open the eggs (see below). Mix with a fork.

2 Use the bridge-cutting technique (see opposite) to cut the tomatoes. Now cut each half into quarters and add to the eggs.

3 Put the butter in a saucepan. Melt over medium (not high) heat. Add the eggs and cook, stirring with a spoon. Keep stirring to break up the egg.

CRACK OPEN THE EGGS

Hold an egg in one hand and carefully use a table knife to crack the egg in the middle. Put your thumbs into the crack and pull the egg shell apart. Let the egg fall into the bowl.

Repeat with the other egg. Fish out any egg shell with a spoon. (See page 60 for a photo of how to crack eggs.)

4 When the eggs are almost cooked (so they look only slightly wet), take the pan off the heat and rest on a stand/trivet. Keep stirring until the eggs are cooked – the heat from the pan will continue to cook them. Eat with toast.

BRIDGE-CUTTING TECHNIQUE

Make a 'bridge' with a thumb and finger of one hand and hold the tomato. Hold a small paring knife in your other hand and put the blade under the bridge, then cut downwards firmly. (See page 56 for a photo of how to do the bridge-cutting technique.)

mini puffy tomato tarts

You'll have great fun when rolling out the pastry, cutting out circles and spreading pesto. If you haven't used a grater before, make sure you keep your fingers away from the sharp 'teeth'.

INGREDIENTS

To make 10 mini tarts you need:

3 big handfuls ripe cherry tomatoes

about 35 g/1 oz. Cheddar cheese

200 g/6½ oz. puff pastry dough

a little flour for sprinkling

4–5 teaspoons pesto
(or sun-dried tomato paste)

you could also try other toppings like chopped olives, chorizo or salami

cutting board • small paring knife grater • pound coin or 2 pennies round cutter about 7 cm/2½ inches across • 2 nonstick baking trays spoon • rolling pin • oven mitts

SKILLS

rolling pastry • cutting circles • spreading choosing toppings • using oven

1 Turn the oven on to 190°C (375°F) Gas 5. Use the bridge-cutting technique to cut the tomatoes: on a cutting board, make a 'bridge' with a thumb and finger of one hand and hold the tomato. Hold a small paring knife in your other hand and put the blade under the bridge, then cut downwards firmly. Now cut each half into quarters.

2 To grate the cheese, hold the handle of the grater with one hand and use the other hand to push the cheese downwards over the grater 'teeth'. Always keep your fingers away from the grater 'teeth' as they are very sharp.

3 Break the dough in half. Sprinkle a little flour on the work surface. Roll one piece of dough with a rolling pin until it is about the same thickness as a pound coin or 2 stacked pennies.

4 Starting at the edge of the dough, push the round cutter down into the dough to cut out circles. Keep going until you have used up both pieces of dough.

5 Put the circles of dough on the baking trays. Use a teaspoon to spread a bit of pesto over each circle. Try to leave a little border around the edge of the circles of dough – this will help the dough to puff up around the pesto when it cooks.

6 Put a few pieces of tomato on top of the pesto and, if you like olives, chorizo or salami, chop some and add those too. Sprinkle the grated cheese over the tarts. Ask an adult to help you put the baking trays into the oven using oven mitts. Cook for 15 minutes. The dough should be cooked and slightly puffy and the cheese will have melted.

pretty prawn cocktails

This is a great lunch, or if you want to have a special meal you could make this for an appetizer. Did you know that prawns/shrimp are grey when they are raw and they turn pink when they are cooked? You can also use melon balls or pineapple chunks for a veggie alternative to prawns.

SKILLS

counting • squeezing lemons • washing vegetables • dividing

INGREDIENTS

For 4 people you need:

4 tablespoons mayonnaise

2 tablespoons tomato ketchup

¼ lemon

about 10 crisp lettuce leaves

250 g/8 oz. cooked, peeled prawns/shrimp

a little paprika

spoon • small bowl • colander
clean kitchen towel
4 small plates or bowls

1 Count the spoons of mayonnaise and ketchup into a small bowl.

2 Squeeze the juice from the lemon quarter into the bowl and mix everything together with the spoon to make a pink sauce.

3 Put the lettuce in a colander and wash in the sink. Gently shake the lettuce to dry it or spread it on a clean kitchen towel to dry out. Tear the lettuce into big chunks.

4 Share the chunks of lettuce between 4 small plates or bowls, then share the prawns/shrimp out evenly too, and put them on top of the lettuce. Spoon a little pink sauce on top of each. Take a small pinch of paprika with your fingers and sprinkle over each bowl.

chunky sandwich

You can make these whenever you have some spare time in the day and then keep them in the fridge until you are ready to cook them. Instead of adding lemon zest to the breadcrumb mixture you could try lime, or to make green fish fingers add lots of fresh chopped herbs to the breadcrumbs. For a veggie option, use halloumi slices instead of fish.

SKILLS

breadcrumbing • cracking eggs • using oven
zesting lemon

INGREDIENTS

For 4 people you need:

8 thin salmon fillets (or white fish like haddock), cut into strips by an adult, or halloumi slices

2 free-range eggs

about 8 tablespoons breadcrumbs

1 unwaxed lemon or lime or handful fresh herbs

8 tablespoons plain/all-purpose flour

8 thick slices bread, some sliced tomatoes and watercress or lettuce

scissors • parchment paper • 2 baking trays • table knife • 3 small bowls spoon • fork • small grater • oven mitts

1 Turn the oven on to 190˚C (375˚F) Gas 5. Cut 2 pieces of parchment paper, each big enough to cover the baking trays. If using fish, rub your finger all over the strips to check for bones. If you feel a sharp bone sticking out, pull it out with your fingers.

2 To crack open the eggs, hold an egg in one hand and carefully use a table knife to crack the egg in the middle. Put your thumbs into the crack and pull the egg shell apart. Let the egg fall into a small bowl. Repeat with the other egg. Fish out any egg shell with a spoon. Mix with a fork.

3 Put the breadcrumbs into a small bowl. To grate the lemon or lime, hold the handle of the grater with one hand and use the other hand to push the fruit downwards over the grater 'teeth'. Always keep your fingers away from the grater 'teeth', as they are very sharp. Add the zest to the breadcrumbs.

4 Count the spoons of flour into a small bowl. Dip all sides of the fish or halloumi first into the flour, then the beaten egg, then the breadcrumbs so that all pieces are well coated. Put the pieces on the baking trays.

5 Ask an adult to help you put the trays into the oven using oven mitts. Bake for 10–15 minutes or until the fish or halloumi is golden and cooked all the way through – ask an adult to help you check this. Ask an adult to help you take the trays out of the oven using oven mitts. Put the pieces inside some bread with sliced tomatoes and watercress.

leftovers couscous

This is a great way to use up leftovers from a big roast dinner – we've used leftover lamb in the pictures. You can also just have fun adding your favourite foods to couscous – try canned fish, crumbled feta cheese, chopped tomatoes, fresh herbs, chopped cucumber, watercress or grated carrot – and then mix it with the salad dressing from page 18 instead of the mint jelly.

SKILLS

preparing couscous • measuring liquid
using scissors • grating

INGREDIENTS

For 4 people you need:

200 g/1⅓ cups couscous

225 ml/1 cup boiling water
(or just enough to cover the couscous)

2 large handfuls dried apricots

1 large courgette/zucchini or 2 small courgettes/zucchini

about 3 teaspoons mint jelly

a few handfuls leftover roast lamb, chopped

freshly ground black pepper, if you like

*heatproof bowl • measuring jug/cups
fork • scissors • grater*

1 Weigh the couscous. How you weigh it will depend on the weighing scales that you use. (See pages 50 and 52 for more information about how to weigh ingredients.) Put the couscous into a heatproof bowl.

2 Ask an adult or older child to boil some water and pour the boiling water into a measuring jug/cup up to the 250-ml/1-cup mark. Pour this water carefully over the couscous. Leave the couscous for about 5 minutes and watch as the hard grains absorb the hot water and become soft and fluffy.

3 Use a fork or your hands to mix the couscous and break up the grains. The grains will feel lovely and soft!

4 Using scissors, snip the apricots into small pieces. To grate the courgette/zucchini, hold the handle of the grater with one hand and use the other hand to push the courgette downwards over the grater 'teeth'. Always keep your fingers away from the grater 'teeth', as they are very sharp. Add the courgettes and apricots to the couscous. Add the mint jelly and chopped roast lamb to the couscous and mix everything together. Taste the mixture and add a little black pepper if you think it needs it.

oven-baked herby burgers

Most people love a good burger and this is a simple recipe for creating your own, you just need to decide whether to go meat or veggie.

SKILLS

chopping with table knife • using scissors
cracking eggs • counting • dividing
shaping • using oven

INGREDIENTS

For 8 small burgers

a little olive or vegetable oil

about 1 oz. (35g) cheddar cheese

small handful fresh herbs e.g. parsley, coriander/cilantro, or thyme

2 spring onions/scallions

1 free-range egg

450 g/1 lb. good-quality minced/ground beef round or sirloin (don't buy extra-lean otherwise your burger will be too dry) or a vegetarian equivalent

8 small burger buns, some lettuce, sliced tomatoes and tomato ketchup

pastry brush • baking sheet table knife cutting board • scissors mixing bowl • small bowl • spoon fork • palette knife • oven mitts

1 Turn the oven on to 190˚C (375˚F) Gas 5. Dip a pastry brush into a little olive or vegetable oil and brush it all over a baking tray. This will stop the burgers from sticking to the tray.

2 Using a table knife, cut the cheese into small pieces on a cutting board.

3 Using scissors, snip the herb into small pieces and put into a mixing bowl. Still using scissors, snip the ends off the spring onions/scallions and throw away, then snip the spring onions into tiny pieces and put in the bowl.

4 Now you need to crack open the egg: hold it in one hand and carefully use a table knife to crack the egg in the middle. Put your thumbs into the crack and pull the egg shell apart. Let the egg fall into a small bowl. Fish out any egg shell with a spoon. (See page 60 for a photo of how to crack eggs.) Mix with a fork.

5 Put the beef, chopped cheese, and egg into the bowl with the herbs and spring onions/scallions and mix everything together really well with your hands.

6 Break the beef mixture in half and then break each piece in half again to make 4 pieces (quarters). Now break each quarter in half again to make 8 pieces (eighths). Roll each piece into a ball with your hands, then put onto the oiled baking sheet and flatten into a burger shape. Do the same with all the pieces. Now, WASH YOUR HANDS – you must always wash your hands thoroughly after handling raw meat.

7 Ask an adult to help you put the sheet into the oven using oven mitts. Cook for 8 minutes. Ask an adult to help you take the sheet out of the oven using oven mitts. Using a palette knife, turn the burgers over and put back in the oven for 8 more minutes or until cooked in the middle. Eat in buns with lettuce, tomatoes and ketchup.

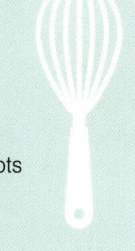

TIP

To make lamb burgers, swap the beef for lamb and add thyme leaves, plus snipped dried apricots instead of cheese.

grilled cheese bagel

Help your parents out by making your own snack or lunch. Just remember that the grill/broiler is hot and you must have an adult with you when you use it. Choose a favourite chutney to spread over the top. If your bagel is for lunch, try to have some chopped cucumber, celery or carrot with it. It is a good idea to have a vegetable or fruit with every meal and snack, so that you eat your '5 a day'.

SKILLS

using grill/broiler
grating • spreading

INGREDIENTS

To make 1 bagel you need:

1 bagel, cut in half

1 slice ham or vegetarian alternative

small piece Cheddar cheese

chutney, if you like

baking tray • grater • oven mitts table knife

1 Turn the grill/broiler on – you will need to ask an adult to show you how to do this, as all grills/broilers are different. Put the bagel halves, cut-side up, onto a baking tray. Tear the ham and put onto the bagel halves around the holes in the middle. Avoid the hole otherwise the ham will fall into it!

2 To grate the cheese, hold the handle of the grater with one hand and use the other hand to push the cheese down over the grater 'teeth'. Keep your fingers away from the grater 'teeth', as they are very sharp. Sprinkle the cheese on the ham.

3 Ask an adult to help you put the baking tray under the grill/broiler using oven mitts. Grill/broil for 3–4 minutes or until the cheese is golden and bubbling. Keep watching it – this will only take a few minutes and if you leave it under the grill/broiler for too long it might burn. Ask an adult to help you take the tray from under the grill/broiler using oven mitts and see how the cheese has melted!

4 Spread a little chutney over the top.

tropical smoothie

Papayas have a green skin that turns yellow as it ripens and the orange flesh is sweet. Passion fruits are small and dark, and their skin wrinkles when it ripens. The skin can be quite tough, so you may need to ask for help with cutting through it. Most smoothies are made using a blender, but they have a very sharp blade that cuts the fruit into tiny pieces, so ask an adult to help you when you use one.

SKILLS

using blender • chopping with paring knife

INGREDIENTS

To make 2 glasses you need:

1 ripe papaya (about 450 g/1 lb.)

1 passion fruit

1 ripe banana

2 small glasses fresh orange juice

cutting board • small paring knife spoon • blender • 2 tall glasses

1 Use the bridge-cutting technique to cut the papaya in half lengthwise: on a cutting board, make a 'bridge' with a thumb and finger of one hand and hold the papaya. Hold a small paring knife in your other hand and put the blade under the bridge, then cut downwards firmly. Cut the passion fruit in half in the same way. You might ask an adult or older child to help you, as passion fruits are quite tough. Using a spoon, scrape the black seeds out of the papaya and throw away.

2 Peel the banana, break it into 2 or 3 pieces and put into the blender. Using a teaspoon, scoop the orange papaya flesh into the blender, too. Now scrape the seeds and juice from the passion fruit on top of the papaya.

3 Pour the orange juice in the blender, put the lid on, and blend until smooth. (Ask an adult or older child to help you.)

4 Pour the smoothie into 2 tall glasses.

lemonberryade

The lemonade without the raspberries will keep for at least a week in a bottle in the fridge. If you do add raspberries, only add them when you are ready to drink the lemonade.

INGREDIENTS

To make 8 glasses you need:

4 lemons

130 g/⅔ cup golden caster/natural cane sugar

1 litre/4 cups cold water

handful fresh raspberries

ice cubes, if you want to make the drink cold!

cutting board • small paring knife lemon juicer • small sieve/strainer jug/pitcher • big spoon • fork measuring jug/cups • small bowl

SKILLS

chopping with paring knife • squeezing lemons pouring • measuring liquids • mashing using sieve/strainer

1 You might like to ask an adult to help you with this, as lemons are quite tough to cut. Use the bridge-cutting technique to cut the lemons: on a cutting board, make a 'bridge' with a thumb and finger of one hand and hold the lemon. Hold a small paring knife in your other hand and put the blade under the bridge, then cut downwards firmly.

2 Put a lemon half over a lemon juicer and press down. Try to turn the lemon as you press down. If you don't have a lemon juicer, you might like to try cutting the lemon half in half again using the bridge-cutting technique to make quarters and then squeeze the lemon quarters with your hands.

3 Before you pour the juice into a jug/pitcher, if there are any seeds in the juice, pour it through a sieve/strainer into the jug/pitcher to catch the seeds.

TIP

If you are going to drink this lemonade as soon as you have made it, you could try using sparkling water to make it fizzy!

4 Add the sugar to the jug/pitcher and stir with a big spoon until the sugar has dissolved (or disappeared).

5 Use a measuring jug/cup to measure 1 litre/4 cups cold water and add to the lemon juice in the jug/pitcher.

6 When you are ready to drink this, put the raspberries in a bowl and mash with a fork. Add them to the lemonade and stir. You need to strain the lemonade again into another jug/pitcher, pushing the raspberries though the sieve/strainer with a fork as you go.

flower & herb ice bowl

I first made one of these at school and I still remember how cool I thought it was to have made my own bowl. You could scoop your favourite ice cream or sorbet into the middle, or just put fresh summer fruits inside. Whatever you choose, I bet your friends will be impressed with the bowl. Remember, you will need to be patient and wait several hours until this is frozen.

INGREDIENTS

To make 1 beautiful ice bowl you need:

fresh edible flowers and/or fresh herbs or any pretty leaves from the garden (we used pink rose petals, rosemary, thyme and sage)

You might like to fill your bowl with a yogurt and fruit mix like the berry crunch on page 40, but you will need to make more to fill your ice bowl (without the cereal). You will also need lots of fresh raspberries and strawberries.

big freezerproof bowl
small freezerproof bowl
small weight • sticky tape
clean kitchen towel • plate

SKILLS

freezing • picking fresh herbs

1 Take your 2 bowls and pour enough cold water into the big bowl to half fill it. Scatter some fresh flowers and/or herbs in the water.

2 Rest the small bowl inside the big bowl and put a small weight in the small bowl to help it sit still. Stretch sticky tape across the tops of the bowls in several directions to hold the small bowl in place inside the big bowl. Put in the freezer and leave overnight.

3 The next day, peel off the sticky tape and carefully pull the small bowl out of the big bowl.

TIP

You might need to sit the big bowl in a little warm water to help ease the ice bowl out of it, but don't leave it sitting in warm water for long otherwise it will melt.

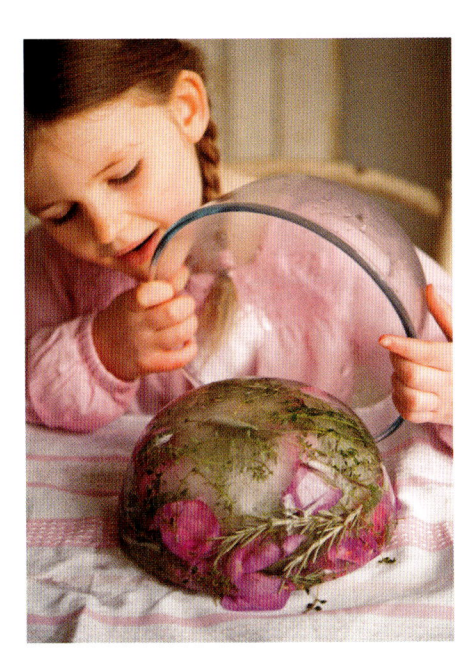

4 Lay a clean kitchen towel on the work surface and tip the big bowl upside down to let the ice bowl slip out. Turn the ice bowl the right way up and sit it on a plate. Fill your ice bowl with the yogurt and fruit mix and top with fresh raspberries and strawberries.

fruit & seed bread

This is easy – you mix the wet ingredients together, then pour them into the dry ingredients. This is half like a cake and half like bread, but you don't need yeast as you do for bread. Look at page 88 for how to make pizza dough using yeast.

SKILLS
greasing • pouring • weighing • measuring • mixing • dividing • using oven

INGREDIENTS

To make 2 small loaves you need:

a little unsalted butter

300 ml/1¼ cups plain yogurt

2 free-range eggs

3 tablespoons sunflower oil

capful vanilla extract

100 g/⅔ cup dried fruit e.g. dried cranberries, raisins or chopped apricots or a mixture of all three

150 g/1 cup chopped nuts, seeds or desiccated coconut or a mixture of all three

250 g/2 cups self-raising/rising flour

125 g/½ cup plus 2 tablespoons golden caster sugar or granulated sugar

1 teaspoon baking powder

parchment paper • 2 x 500-g/1-lb. loaf tins/pans • scissors • table knife small bowl • spoon • fork • measuring jug/cup • mixing bowl • wooden spoon oven mitts • skewer

1 Turn the oven on to 180°C (350°F) Gas 4. Using a scrap of parchment paper, rub a little butter inside the loaf tins/pans. Using scissors, cut a piece of parchment paper to fit along the bottoms of the tins and up the ends. Fit it inside the tins – this will make it easy to pull the bread out after it's baked.

2 Spoon the yogurt into a measuring jug/cup and stop when the yogurt reaches the 300-ml/1¼-cup mark on the jug/cup.

3 Crack open the eggs: hold an egg in one hand and carefully use a table knife to crack the egg in the middle. Put your thumbs into the crack and pull the egg shell apart. Let the egg fall into a bowl. Repeat with the other egg. Fish out any egg shell with a spoon. (See page 60 for a photo of how to crack eggs.) Mix with a fork. Add the eggs, sunflower oil and vanilla to the yogurt and mix with a fork.

4 Weigh the dried fruit, nuts, flour and sugar. How you weigh them will depend on the weighing scales you use. (See pages 50 and 52 for more information about how to weigh ingredients.)

5 Put all the weighed dry ingredients – dried fruit, nuts, flour and sugar – into a mixing bowl. Add the baking powder and mix together. Pour the yogurt mixture into the mixing bowl, too.

6 Use the wooden spoon to mix everything together. Spoon half the mixture into one loaf tin/pan and the other half into the other tin. Ask an adult to help you put the loaf tins in the oven using oven mitts. Bake for about 30 minutes, or until golden and risen.

7 Ask an adult to help you test if the breads are cooked by poking the middle with a skewer – it should come out clean. Let the breads cool down until they're cool enough to touch. Pull the ends of the parchment paper up at each end of the loaf tins and pull the bread out.

shortbread shapes

If you want to bake and you don't have many ingredients in the cupboard, this is a great recipe to make. When you choose cutters, make sure they are about the same size, because if you put big shortbreads onto a baking tray with little shortbreads, the little ones will be cooked a long time before the big ones! This recipe makes a lot of shapes – the number will depend on the size of the cutters you use.

SKILLS

creaming • rolling • cutting • using oven

INGREDIENTS

To make lots of shortbread shapes you need:

125 g/1 stick unsalted butter, soft

55 g/¼ cup golden caster sugar/natural cane sugar plus a little extra

capful vanilla extract

175 g/1⅓ cups plain/all-purpose flour

1 tablespoon milk

scissors • parchment paper
baking tray • mixing bowl
wooden spoon • rolling pin
pound coin or 2 pennies
shaped cutters • fork • oven mitts

1 Turn the oven on to 190°C (375°F) Gas 5. Cut a piece of parchment paper big enough to cover the baking tray.

2 Put the soft butter, sugar and vanilla extract in a mixing bowl and mix well with a wooden spoon until it becomes fluffy and paler in colour. This helps to beat air into the mixture.

3 Add the flour and milk to the bowl and mix until the mixture comes together to form a ball. You can do this with your hands or the wooden spoon.

4 Break the dough into 3 pieces. Sprinkle a little flour over the work surface and the rolling pin. Flatten one piece of dough with a rolling pin until it is the same thickness as a pound coin or 2 stacked pennies. Take the cutters you have chosen and, starting at the edge of the dough, push them down into the dough to cut out shapes. Repeat with the rest of the dough.

5 Carefully lift the shapes onto the baking tray, then press a fork gently onto the shortbread to make pretty patterns. Sprinkle a little sugar over the top of the shortbread. Ask an adult to help you put the sheet in the oven using oven mitts. Bake for 10 minutes (if they are small shapes) or 15 minutes (if they are big shapes), or until golden.

what's-in-season fruit crumble

One of the first things my mum taught me to make was a crumble. It's a great way to learn how to rub butter into flour. Once you know how to do this you can have a go at making pastry (see page 114). Try to choose fruit that is in season – if you are not sure what that is, ask the person working in the produce section of your supermarket or go to a local farmers' market.

SKILLS

rubbing in • cutting with knife
mixing with spoon • sprinkling topping

(see page 114)

INGREDIENTS

For 4–6 people you need:

FRUIT FILLING

seasonal fruit, e.g. 15 plums or about 600 g/1 lb. 4 oz. fresh or frozen berries or about 12 peaches or nectarines

4 tablespoons orange juice

3 tablespoons light brown sugar

1 tablespoon plain/all-purpose flour

CRUMBLE TOPPING

150 g/1 cup plus 2 tablespoons plain/all-purpose flour

100 g/6½ tablespoons unsalted butter, chilled and cut into small pieces

2 handfuls oats (or muesli if you prefer)

4 tablespoons light brown sugar

1 teaspoon ground mixed spice/apple pie spice or ground cinnamon

cutting board • small paring knife spoon • 2 small or 1 large ovenproof dishes

1 Turn the oven on to 180˚C (350˚F) Gas 4. To make the fruit filling, use the bridge-cutting technique to cut the plums in half: on a cutting board, make a 'bridge' with a thumb and finger of one hand and hold the plum. Hold a small paring knife in your other hand and put the blade under the bridge, then cut downwards firmly. Move the plums around as you cut to avoid cutting through the stone. Take out the stones.

2 Put the plums into 2 small or 1 large ovenproof dish. Pour the orange juice over the plums, add the sugar and flour, and mix with a spoon or your hands.

3 To make the crumble topping, put the flour into a bowl, add the butter, and rub the butter into the flour with your fingers until it looks like fine breadcrumbs (see page 114 for photos showing you how to do this). This can take a few minutes. Add the oats, sugar and spice and mix with your fingers again.

4 Spoon the mixture over the top of the plums. Ask an adult to help you put the dishes into the oven using oven mitts. Bake for 25–30 minutes, or until the crumble topping is crisp, the plums are soft and the fruit juices are bubbling up around the edges.

marshmallow & chocolate squares

This is only to be eaten occasionally, as it is very sweet! Remember, you will need to be patient while you wait for it to set.

SKILLS

melting chocolate • mixing • setting in fridge

INGREDIENTS

To make about 30 small pieces you need:

12 digestive biscuits/graham crackers or ginger biscuits/cookies

50 g/¾ cup mini-marshmallows

150 g/1 cup dried fruit e.g. raisins, chopped mango, chopped apricots

100 g/3½ oz. milk chocolate

100 g/6½ oz. unsalted butter, chopped into big chunks

5 tablespoons golden/corn syrup

mixing bowl • large saucepan teaspoon • wooden spoon • parchment paper • any cake tin/pan (round, square or loaf tin) • scissors • table knife

1 Using a scrap of parchment paper, rub a little butter inside the cake tin/pan. Now using scissors, cut a piece of parchment to fit along the bottom of the tin and up the ends. Fit it inside the tin. Put the digestive biscuits/graham crackers into a mixing bowl. Break them into small pieces. Add the mini-marshmallows and dried fruit.

2 Break the chocolate into small pieces and put into a large saucepan with the butter. Add the golden/corn syrup – you might need to use a teaspoon to scrape the syrup off the tablespoon.

3 Ask an adult to help you turn the hob/burner onto low heat and put the saucepan over it. Leave for a few minutes until the chocolate starts to melt. Stir with a wooden spoon until the mixture is smooth. Take the pan off the heat, add the fruit and stir everything together.

4 Spoon the mixture into the tin/pan and push it down with the spoon. Cover with parchment paper and put in the fridge for 4 hours or until hard – be patient while you wait for it to set. Pull the ends of the parchment paper up at each end of the tin and pull the mixture out – you may need to run a table knife along the sides to help release it from the tin. Cut into small pieces and put into a jar.

bumblebee cakes

Have you ever made butterfly cakes? My children and their friends have made a variation of the butterfly cake, the bumblebee. It's flavoured with orange, but you could just add vanilla if you prefer. Make them plain or with cocoa powder.

SKILLS

creaming butter & sugar • cracking eggs
folding flour

INGREDIENTS

To make 10 bumblebee cakes you need:

CAKES

½ orange

125 g/1 stick unsalted butter, soft

125 g/1 generous cup golden caster sugar/natural cane sugar

capful vanilla extract

2 free-range eggs

125 g/1 cup self-raising/rising flour OR if you want to make them chocolatey use 100 g/¾ cup self-raising/rising flour and 25 g/¼ cup cocoa powder

BUTTERCREAM

½ orange

50 g/3 tablespoons unsalted butter, soft

125 g/1 scant cup icing/confectioners' sugar

TO DECORATE

chocolate buttons and chocolate matchsticks (or long thin sweets/candies)

mixing bowl • wooden spoon table knife • 2 bowls • large metal spoon • 12-hole cupcake tin/pan lined with 12 paper cases

1 Turn the oven on to 180˚C (350˚F) Gas 4. To make the cakes, squeeze the juice from the orange half into a mixing bowl and add the soft butter, sugar and vanilla extract. Mix well with a wooden spoon until it becomes fluffy and paler in colour. This helps to beat air into the mixture. Crack open the eggs: hold an egg in one hand and use a table knife to crack the egg in the middle. Put your thumbs into the crack and pull the egg shell apart. Let the egg fall into a bowl. Repeat with the other egg. Fish out any egg shell with a spoon. (See page 60 for a photo of how to crack eggs.)

2 Add the eggs to the butter mixture and beat. Add the flour and 'fold' in (see page 51) with a metal spoon.

3 Divide the batter evenly between the cupcake cases with a spoon. Ask an adult to help you put the tin/pan in the oven using oven mitts. Bake for about 12–15 minutes until golden and slightly springy to the touch. Ask an adult to help you take the tin out of the oven using oven mitts and let cool.

4 Using a table knife, cut a small oval shape from the middle of each cake. Cut this oval in half to make 2 wings.

5 To make the buttercream, squeeze the orange half into a bowl. Add the soft butter and sugar and mix well.

6 Spoon this into the holes in each cupcake, then stick the wings into the buttercream. Stick chocolate buttons and matchsticks into the cakes to make them look like bumblebees.

Stage 3: 7-11 years

grown-ups: this page is for you

children: you can skip this bit and have fun cooking!

This age range is huge. Some children will be able to cook independently and others will still need some assistance. But here are a few things that your child will be beginning to do during this stage. Remind your child that she can go back to Stage 1 of the book as she will find those recipes easy to make.

• It is likely that your child will be well into the swing of following the recipes on his own by now, and will be gaining independence and confidence in the kitchen. This is what this book is all about!

• She will enjoy the chance to try new pieces of kitchen equipment. Try to stand back and let her feel that she is in control, at the same time being nearby if help is needed. It is very easy to take over in the kitchen, so try to hold back.

• By now, most children like to cook with a friend or sibling. The sooner children realize that cooking is a fun and sociable activity, the better!

• He will have an increased ability to remember and should be able to easily repeat skills from the previous chapters. These new skills will be with him now for life.

• Her coordination will be greatly improved and she will have more control over smaller muscles, making it easier to complete more intricate tasks.

• He will be able to plan ahead more easily, for example if he is helping to make a meal, he will have a better understanding of timing and planning.

• She is likely to be keen to understand more about the science behind food, for example about yeast and kneading, and about cake making.

• Children at this age still enjoy learning through play, which is just one reason why cooking is so great, as he can learn essential life skills while having fun in the kitchen.

• She will be able to start to teach other family members her new-found skills.

• Some children will be ready to cook a two- or even three-course meal for the family using the recipes from all the stages in this book – enjoy being cooked for!

• Make sure he helps to clear up after he has finished cooking! This is a really important life skill.

skills

Here are more skills that you can learn and practise as you make the recipes in this chapter. You will also be using some skills from the previous chapters, but they will be so easy by now that you probably won't even realize you are using them.

peeling vegetables

Hold the fruit or vegetable in one hand and the peeler in the other hand. Press it onto the fruit or vegetable and push away from you. It is a good idea to practise peeling vegetables with different peelers to see which you find the easiest; there are lots of different kinds and some are easier to use than others.

kneading dough

This means to bash and push the dough. This helps to move the yeast cells around the dough and makes it stretchy. You may need to knead for 10 minutes before the dough is ready. It should be smooth, stretchy and almost silky when you touch it. To test if the dough has been kneaded for long enough, roll it into a ball and prod it with your finger – it should spring back quickly.

making a white sauce

This is a great skill to learn, as once you know how to make a white sauce, you can then make a pasta meal for your family like the swirly pasta with leek, broccoli & cheese sauce on page 96. The best method is to make a 'roux', which is when you melt the butter in the pan, add the flour and then cook the flour and butter mixture to make a paste or 'roux'. You then add the milk to the paste and keep cooking. However, you can also try putting all the ingredients into the pan together. Use a balloon whisk to keep stirring the mixture over gentle heat until you have a smooth sauce. This is the 'all in one' method.

cooking basmati rice

This type of rice grows in India. You always want to use twice as much volume of water as rice. This means that if you want to cook 1 mug/cup of rice, you will need 2 mugs/cups of water. Put the rice and water into a saucepan and cover with the lid. Bring to a boil and then lower the heat under the pan until the rice is simmering. Cook for 14 minutes, then very carefully take the pan off the heat and stand it on a heatproof pan stand/trivet for 10 minutes. You should have white, fluffy rice at the end.

rolling up sushi

This is great fun and gets easier the more you practice. Gently roll the seaweed around the rice and filling and gently press together.

ladling

Sometimes it is easiest to use a ladle to transfer food like stew or soup from one container to another. A ladle is like a small bowl with a handle.

Kneading dough

Rolling up sushi

bashing garlic

If you don't have a garlic press or if you prefer to keep the garlic clove whole – like for the lemony chicken recipe on page 110 – you can always just squash the garlic slightly to release some of its juices and flavour and keep it whole. Bash the clove of garlic with the end of a rolling pin to loosen the papery skin. Peel off the skin and throw away. Now bash the clove again with the end of the rolling pin to split the garlic slightly. Remember to wash the rolling pin.

baking potatoes

Always prick the potatoes with a fork first and bake them in a very hot oven so that the skins are crisp and the insides are soft and fluffy.

separating eggs

This is when you want to separate the yolks and the whites in the eggs. There are different ways to do this. For example, take 2 bowls. Crack the egg over one bowl and then carefully tip the white and yolk from one shell half into the other. As you move the egg between the shells, let the white gradually drop into the bowl until you're just left with the yolk in the egg shell. Now drop the yolk into the second bowl. Alternatively, you may prefer to crack the egg onto a saucer and then cover the yolk with a small bowl. Tip the saucer so that the white drips into a bowl, leaving the yolk behind on the saucer.

roasting

To roast something in the oven means to cook it at a high temperature with only a little fat, like olive oil.

cooking pasta

You will need the biggest pan that you can find so that the pasta has plenty of room to move around in the water as it cooks. This will help to make sure that it cooks evenly. See page 94 for more information about how to cook pasta.

draining

You will need an adult or older child to help you drain pasta, as the saucepan will be heavy and the water will be very hot. Try to wear oven mitts to help prevent the water from splashing on your hands. Rest the colander in the sink and then very carefully pour the pasta and hot water into the colander.

marinating

A marinade can be made from a variety of ingredients, but it often contains an acid like lemon juice and an oil, plus a few other ingredients to add flavour. Add the meat or fish and leave to marinate for a little while to make sure that the flavours soak into the food before you cook it. The marinade will help to keep the meat or fish juicy as it cooks.

whisking egg whites

If you are using a balloon whisk to whisk egg whites, you might need to pass the whisk to a friend and take it in turns to stop your wrist from aching. If you use an electric mixer, it is much quicker!

why do cakes rise?

When you beat together the butter and sugar and then beat in the eggs, you are adding air to the batter. When you bake the cake, the air inside the bubbles gets bigger, helping the cake to rise. Many cakes use self-raising/rising flour and sometimes baking powder too. These both contain carbon dioxide, which is released as a gas when it is heated. As the carbon dioxide becomes a gas, it gets bigger and pushes the cake up, making it rise.

melting chocolate

Find a small bowl that will sit on top of a saucepan so that the bottom of the bowl is just under the rim of the pan. Break the chocolate into small pieces (this helps it to melt quickly and evenly) and put into the small bowl. Half fill the saucepan with water, put the bowl of chocolate on top and bring it to a gentle simmer. Leave for a few minutes, then turn the heat off. Stir the chocolate carefully until it has melted. If the chocolate gets too hot, the cocoa butter will begin to separate from the cocoa solids, and the chocolate can become dry and crumbly. It is really important that you do not let any liquid like water drip into the chocolate – even a tiny amount can cause the chocolate to harden and turn into a solid lump! If this happens you will need to start again.

setting a table for a meal

If you are serving a starter and a main course, you will need to lay two sets of cutlery at the table. Put the knife and fork on the table as normal and then lay a smaller knife and fork on the outside of this cutlery for the appetizer. When you eat a meal with more than one course, start with the cutlery on the outside and work your way into the middle.

kitchen equipment

You have already used most of the basic kitchen utensils, but there are just a few other utensils that are worth mentioning in case you choose to cook all the recipes in this chapter.

whisks

You will need either a balloon whisk or an electric mixer to whisk egg whites until they are white and fluffy. I always recommend that if possible you have a go at whisking with a balloon whisk to practise how to whisk. You can always use an electric mixer later to see the difference.

small pudding basins

These are good to have for making small baked desserts or you could use them for setting jellies. You might also hear an adult suggest that you use ramekins. These are small dishes that can be put into the oven.

vegetable peeler

These can be quite tricky to use, so you may need to have a go with friends' peelers until you find one that you are happy with.

small grater

Some big graters have small holes on them that you can use for grating ingredients that you want to make tiny pieces from. If your big grater doesn't have small enough holes, you will need a small grater.

pan stand/trivet

As it sounds, this is a small heatproof stand for resting hot pans on. It is very handy to have a pan stand/trivet by the hob/stovetop. You can then take something out of the oven and put it on the stand/trivet. Never put anything hot onto the kitchen work surface, as you might damage the surface.

pasta pan

A pasta pan has its own colander inside the pan, ready for draining the pasta when it is cooked. Most Italians have a pasta pan, as they cook pasta a lot. It doesn't matter if you don't have one – just use a large pan and a colander instead. (Always ask an adult to drain the pasta for you, as the pan will be heavy and full of boiling water.)

wok or frying pan/skillet

Now that you are used to cooking on the hob/stovetop, you might like to try making the stir-fry on page 92. The best pan for a stir-fry is a wok, as it is large enough to give you space to toss the vegetables around and 'stir' them as you 'fry'. If you don't have a wok, you could use a large frying pan/skillet.

fluted cutters

Some cook stores sell these individually, or you could buy a set so that you have different-sized cutters to play with.

roasting dish

Ideally you need a heavy-based roasting dish. This will heat up and cook the food without burning it.

12-hole cupcake tin/pan

This tin is ideal for making small cakes or tarts. Once you know how to make pastry, you can make your own recipe.

2 x 20-cm/8-inch cake tins/pans

If you only have one cake tin/pan and you want to make a layer cake like a Victoria sponge where you sandwich 2 cakes together, you need to make half the batter and bake it, then make the other half and bake it. Or you can see if a neighbour or friend has another cake tin you could use.

sushi mat or napkin

If you don't have to have a sushi mat, you can use a napkin instead. A sushi mat is used to roll the sushi into a long sausage shape.

bowls for marinating

When you marinate fish, meat or vegetables, put the marinade ingredients in a glass, Pyrex, melamine or plastic bowl, not a metal one. Acidic ingredients like lemon juice and vinegar can react with the metal and give the food a funny taste.

Whisk

Pudding basins

Small grater

Wok

Frying pan

Fluted cutter

12-hole cupcake tin/pan

Cake tins/pans

Sushi mat

ham & pineapple pizzas

Did you know that yeast is alive? It is a living micro-organism used to make bread rise and give it a lighter, more open texture. For the yeast to work, it needs warmth (from warm water), moisture (water) and food (sugar from the flour). The yeast produces a gas, carbon dioxide, which makes the bread rise before it is baked. You can swap the ham for a veggie alternative if you prefer.

SKILLS

making yeast dough • rolling • spreading using oven

INGREDIENTS

To make 2 very large or 3–4 small pizzas you need:

PIZZA DOUGH

350 g/2¾ cups strong plain white flour/all-purpose flour

7-g packet/1¼ teaspoons 'easy bake'/instant yeast

2 tablespoons olive oil plus a little extra

200 ml/1 scant cup warm (not hot) water

TOPPINGS

tomato passata/purée, ham, pineapple, mozzarella and grated cheese OR tomato passata/purée, prawns/shrimp and sliced (bell) peppers OR any other topping combinations that you might like to try

mixing bowl • measuring jug/cup wooden spoon • clingfilm/plastic wrap pastry brush • 2 baking trays rolling pin • spoon • oven mitts

1 Put the flour into a mixing bowl. Sprinkle the yeast over the top. Make a well (a hole) in the middle of the flour with your hand.

2 Pour the warm water into a measuring jug/cup until it just reaches the 200-ml/1-cup mark. Make sure the water is warm and not too hot – when you put your finger in, it should feel just warm. Add the olive oil to the water, then pour into the well. Use a wooden spoon to stir the liquid and the flour will gradually fall into the water. Keep stirring until all the flour is mixed with the liquid and you have a dough.

3 Sprinkle a little flour over the work surface, take the dough out of the bowl and knead it. The best way to knead is to push the dough down and away with the heel of the hand and then pull it back with your fingers. Push it back onto the work surface, turn the dough slightly and then repeat. After a few minutes of doing this, the dough should have a smooth, elastic texture.

DID YOU KNOW?

Kneading the dough helps to distribute the yeast cells evenly and give the dough elasticity (which means it is stretchy). You may need to knead for up to 10 minutes before the dough is smooth, elastic and almost silky to touch. To test if the dough has been kneaded for long enough, roll it into a ball and prod it with your finger – it should spring back quickly.

4 Clean the mixing bowl and put the dough back in. Cover it with clingfilm/plastic wrap or a clean kitchen towel and leave it somewhere warm to rise for about an hour, or until it is twice as big – look how much the dough has grown in the picture!

5 Turn the oven on to 200°C (400°F) Gas 6. Dip a pastry brush into a little olive oil and brush it all over the baking trays. Break the risen dough in half and, using a rolling pin, roll each piece into two large flat circles.

6 Lift the pizza crusts onto the baking trays. Spread the tomato passata/purée over the crusts with the back of a spoon.

7 Scatter your ham and pineapple over the tomato passata/purée. Using oven mitts, put the trays in the oven and bake for 15–20 minutes or until the crusts are cooked.

tacos with soya beans

The mild chilli powder in this recipe gives the beans a slight chilli flavour, but you can always leave it out if you really don't like it – they will still taste good. This simple meal is as fun to make as it is to eat because there are lots of things to assemble, and so lots of things to try!

SKILLS

**opening cans • cutting • crushing garlic
using hob/stovetop and oven**

INGREDIENTS

For 4 people you need:

400 g/14 oz. canned chopped tomatoes

2 x 400-g/14-oz. cans soya/soybeans in water (or cannellini/pinto beans)

2 spring onions/scallions

1 garlic clove

1 tablespoon olive oil

1 teaspoon ground coriander

1 teaspoon mild chilli powder

1 teaspoon sugar

handful coriander/cilantro leaves plus a little extra

8–12 tacos

2 ripe avocados

150 ml/⅔ cup sour cream

grated Cheddar cheese

pieces of lime

*can opener • colander
small paring knife • cutting board
garlic press • small saucepan
wooden spoon • baking tray
oven mitts • spoon*

1 Turn the oven on to 180°C (350°F) Gas 4. Use a can opener to open the cans of tomatoes and beans. The first time you do this you will need an adult to show you how to use your can opener, as they are all slightly different. Drain the beans in a colander.

2 Using the claw-cutting technique (see page 50), cut the ends off the spring onions/scallions with a small paring knife and throw away. Cut the spring onions into thin slices.

3 Peel the garlic clove and crush it with a garlic press.

4 Put the oil and spring onions/scallions into a small pan over low heat on the hob/stovetop. Heat gently for about 5 minutes, stirring every now and then with a wooden spoon, until they are soft. Add the crushed garlic, ground coriander and chilli powder and cook for another minute.

5 Add the tomatoes, drained beans, sugar and coriander/cilantro leaves. Turn the heat up. When the tomatoes are bubbling, lower the heat and let simmer gently for 10 minutes.

6 Put the tacos on a baking tray and, using oven mitts, put them in the oven for 3 minutes to heat up. Scoop the stones out of the avocados with a teaspoon and peel away the skins. Using the claw-cutting technique, cut the avocados into slices. Put the beans, sour cream, cheese, extra coriander/cilantro, avocado and lime in bowls. Let everyone make their own tacos.

tacos with soya beans 91

rainbow stir-fry

I have used ready-prepared vegetables here so all you need to prepare are the leeks and green beans. When you have practised using a small sharp knife, you may like to add other vegetables like sliced red or yellow (bell) peppers or bok choy.

SKILLS

knife skills • stir-frying • grating
crushing garlic • preparing vegetables

INGREDIENTS

For 4 people you need:

1 leek, trimmed and washed

about 200 g/1½ cups green beans

2 large handfuls coriander/cilantro leaves

2 garlic cloves

small piece ginger, about 2.5 cm/1 inch

2 teaspoons sesame oil

2 teaspoons olive oil

about 300 g/10 oz. crunchy vegetable stir-fry mix (package sizes will vary; the amount doesn't have to be exact)

300 g/10 oz. pre-cooked free-range egg noodles

2 large handfuls pine nuts or peanuts, if you like

1–2 tablespoons low-salt soy sauce

small paring knife • cutting board
scissors • garlic press • small grater
wok or large frying pan/skillet
wooden spoon

1 Use the bridge-cutting technique to cut the leeks in half widthwise, then lengthwise with a small paring knife. Using the claw-cutting technique, thinly slice the leeks.

2 Using scissors, snip the coriander/cilantro into small pieces. Still using scissors, cut the ends off the beans and throw them away. Cut the beans in half.

3 Peel the garlic clove and crush it with a garlic press. Grate the ginger using a small grater (you don't need to peel it first).

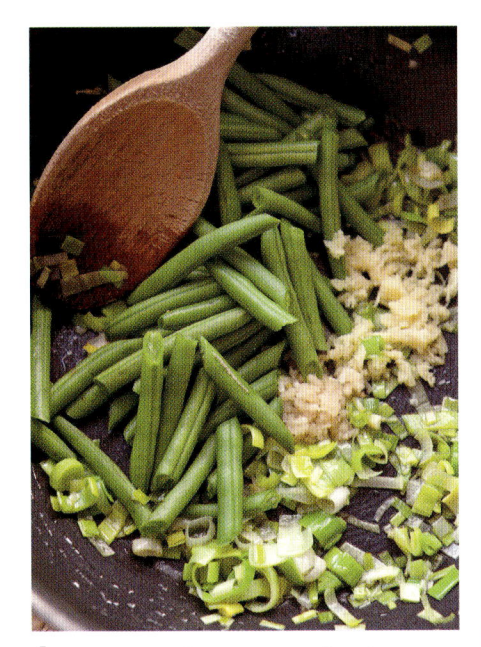

4 Turn the hob/burner to medium heat. Heat the oils in a wok or large frying pan/skillet. Add the leeks and fry for a few minutes, stirring with a wooden spoon. Add the garlic, ginger and beans and fry for another minute.

5 Add the vegetable stir-fry mix and fry for another minute. Add the noodles, coriander/cilantro, nuts and soy sauce and fry for a few minutes, stirring as you fry.

how to cook pasta

Knowing how to cook pasta is a great skill, as it is so easy to make it into a lovely meal. However, you will need help from an adult, as the pasta pan will be very heavy and full of hot water!

INGREDIENTS

For 1 person you need:
75–115 g/2½–4 oz. dried pasta

the biggest saucepan you have
jug/pitcher
long-handled or wooden spoon

1 Ideally you need 1 litre/4 cups of water for every 100 g/3½ oz. pasta, but this will only work if you have a pan big enough for this amount of water. However, only ever fill your saucepan three-quarters full. Don't fill it to the top or it will overflow when you add the pasta!

2 Find the biggest saucepan that you have in your kitchen (the pasta needs to be cooked in a large pan to help make sure that it cooks evenly; if the pan is too small, some of the pasta may be trapped at the bottom of the pan and it will cook more quickly than the pasta at the top). Turn the hob/burner to medium heat and put the pan of water on it. Heat the water until it comes to a boil – you will know that it is boiling when you can see the water bubbling.

3 Put your pasta into a jug/pitcher and then carefully add the pasta to the water (keep your hands away from the hot water!). Using a long-handled spoon, gently swirl the pasta around in the pan to help stop it from sticking together. Bring the water back to a boil and cook following the packet instructions (all pastas have different cooking times). Use a fork to take a piece of pasta from the pan, let cool slightly and then test to see if it is ready: when you bite into it, it should be cooked but still have a little 'bite' – this is known as 'al dente' in Italy. When it is cooked, put a colander in the sink and ask an adult to pour the pasta into the colander for you (remember, the pan will be very heavy) to drain it.

pasta sauces

pepper pasta sauce

You need to use just plain roasted (bell) peppers for this recipe, not antipasti peppers that have lots of oils and herbs added to them.

INGREDIENTS

For 4 people you need:

10 oz. roasted red (bell) peppers from a jar

300 g/10 oz. pasta shapes, cooked and drained (see opposite for instructions)

handful fresh basil or coriander/cilantro leaves

handful baby spinach leaves

4 tablespoons cream cheese

colander • scissors • saucepan wooden spoon

Drain the roasted peppers in a colander in the sink. Using scissors, snip the peppers into really small pieces (the smaller the better) and add to the cooked and drained pasta in the saucepan. Tear the basil or coriander/cilantro leaves and spinach into small pieces and add to the pasta with the cream cheese. Put the pan over low heat and cook until the cream cheese has melted, stirring gently with a wooden spoon.

tuna pasta sauce

This is a great quick supper and good for packed lunches too. Swap the tuna for chickpeas for a veggie alternative.

INGREDIENTS

For 4 people you need:

150 g/1 cup canned or frozen (and defrosted) sweetcorn/corn kernels

2 x 185-g/6-oz. cans tuna, drained

3–4 tablespoons mayonnaise

300 g/10 oz. pasta shapes, cooked and drained (see opposite for instructions)

can opener • colander • bowl fork • spoon

Use a can opener to open the can of sweetcorn/corn kernels. The first time you do this you will need an adult to show you how to use your can opener, as they all differ slightly. If you are using frozen corn, you will need to let it defrost for at least 1 hour before you make the pasta sauce. Use the can opener to open the cans of tuna. Drain both the corn and tuna in a colander, then tip into a bowl. Break the tuna up with a fork, add the mayonnaise and mix. Spoon the mixture over the cooked pasta and mix well.

swirly pasta with leek, broccoli & cheese sauce

It's useful to know how to make a white sauce like this one because it is used in many dishes like lasagne, mac and cheese and cauliflower cheese.

SKILLS

chopping • making white sauce • cooking pasta using oven

INGREDIENTS

For 4 people you need:

300 g/10 oz. tenderstem broccoli/broccolini

1 leek, trimmed and washed

50 g/3 tablespoons unsalted butter

50 g/⅓ cup plain/all-purpose flour

500 ml/2 cups whole milk

1 teaspoon English mustard

2 large handfuls grated Cheddar or hard cheese

250 g/8 oz. pasta spirals

small paring knife • cutting board saucepan • wooden spoon • balloon whisk • colander • ovenproof dish oven mitts

1 Turn the oven on to 190˚C (375˚F) Gas 5. Use the claw-cutting technique to cut the broccoli into chunks with a small paring knife. Using the same technique, slice the leek into thin slices.

2 Turn the hob/burner onto a low heat. Put the leek and butter into a saucepan and heat gently. Cook for about 10 minutes, or until the leek has softened. Stir with a wooden spoon. Add the flour.

3 Stir and cook for a few minutes until you have a thick paste. Now take a balloon whisk and, whisking all the time, slowly pour in the milk. Keep whisking until you have a smooth sauce and cook gently for a few minutes. Add the mustard and almost all the cheese (keep some for the top) to the sauce, stir and take off the heat.

4 Cook the pasta following the instructions on page 94. Add the broccoli to the pasta pan 2 minutes before the pasta has finished cooking. When it is cooked, put a colander in the sink and ask an adult to pour the pasta and broccoli into the colander for you. Tip the pasta and broccoli from the colander into an ovenproof dish. Pour the sauce over the top and sprinkle the last bit of cheese over it. Using oven mitts, put the dish in the oven. Cook for 25–30 minutes until the topping is golden and the sauce is bubbling.

swirly pasta with leek, broccoli & cheese sauce 97

easy minestrone soup

Minestrone is a tasty, thick soup that can be made with a variety of ingredients, including onions, carrots, celery, potatoes, cabbage, tomatoes, legumes (such as beans, chickpeas, or fava beans), pasta and rice. The great thing about this soup is that you don't have to blend it at the end of cooking. It's ready to eat just as it is, all lovely and chunky.

SKILLS

cutting • using stovetop • crushing garlic using scissors

INGREDIENTS

For 4 people you need:

4 spring onions/scallions

1 garlic clove

1 tablespoon olive oil

500g/2 cups passata/tomato purée

1 teaspoon sugar

390-g/14-oz. can soya/soybeans in water

100 g/¾ cup small pasta for soup

2 large handfuls frozen peas

2 tablespoons pesto

handful grated Parmesan

small paring knife • cutting board rolling pin • garlic press heavy-based saucepan • wooden spoon

1 Using the claw-cutting technique, cut the ends off the spring onions/scallions with a small paring knife and throw away. Now slice the spring onions/scallions into thin slices.

2 Bash the garlic clove with a rolling pin, then peel off the skin.

3 Crush the garlic using a garlic press.

TIP

To add green beans instead of peas, cut the ends off using scissors, then cut the beans into small pieces before you put them into the soup.

4 Turn the hob/burner to low heat. Heat the oil in a heavy-based saucepan. Fry the spring onions/scallions and garlic for 2 minutes, stirring occasionally with a wooden spoon. Pour the passata/tomato purée into the pan. Fill the tomato container with water and pour into the pan. Do this twice. Add the sugar.

5 Add the beans. Turn the heat up to high and cook until the mixture is simmering. Lower the heat and simmer gently for 15 minutes.

6 Add the pasta, peas and pesto and cook for another 5 minutes (or however long the pasta packet says). Sprinkle the grated Parmesan on top.

fish curry with rice

Have you ever been to a curry house? You may think that all curries are hot and spicy, but they are not. They can be mild and creamy and taste delicious like this. For a vegetarian meal, swap the fish out for more vegetables.

SKILLS
chopping • cooking rice • simmering using hob/stovetop

INGREDIENTS

For 4 people you need:

big handful coriander/cilantro leaves

3 spring onions/scallions

1 tablespoon olive oil

3 tablespoons mild curry paste

400 g/14 oz. canned chopped tomatoes

200 ml/1 scant cup hot vegetable stock or hot water

large handful few different vegetables e.g. baby corn and green beans

300 g/10 oz. mixed fresh fish fillets e.g. haddock, salmon, monkfish, cut into big chunks, or raw peeled prawns/shrimp

cooked long-grain rice (see opposite for instructions)

naan bread, poppadoms and mango chutney, to serve

scissors • small paring knife
cutting board • large saucepan
wooden spoon

1 Using scissors, snip the coriander/cilantro into small pieces. Using the bridge-cutting technique, slice the vegetables in half lengthwise with a small paring knife. Using the claw-cutting technique, cut the ends off the spring onions/scallions. Cut the spring onions into thin slices. Turn the hob/burner to low heat. Put the spring onions and oil in a large saucepan on the hob/stovetop and heat gently.

2 Add the curry paste and fry for a few minutes, stirring with a wooden spoon.

3 Add the canned tomatoes to the pan, then fill the can with the hot stock or water and add to the pan, too. Simmer for 10 minutes, stirring once or twice.

4 Add the vegetables and cook for 5 minutes. Add the fish and cook until it is cooked – this will only be 5 minutes as you don't want to overcook it. Ask an adult to help you check if it is cooked. Add the coriander/cilantro and stir. Serve with rice, naan, poppadoms and chutney.

how to cook rice

Knowing how to cook rice is a great skill, as it can be used in so many meals. However, you will need help from an adult, as the rice pan will be very heavy and full of hot water!

INGREDIENTS

For 2 people you need:
1 tall glass of long-grain rice

tall glass • saucepan

1 Measure 1 tall glass or cup of rice. Put the rice and then 2 glasses of water into a saucepan. Turn the hob/burner to medium heat and put the pan on the hob/stovetop.

2 Bring the water in the pan up to a boil, lower the heat, put the lid on the pan and simmer for 14 minutes. Ask an adult to help you take the pan off the hob/stovetop and leave for 10 minutes with the lid on. The rice will continue to steam and become fluffy. Don't take the lid off during this time – it is important that the lid stays on if you want fluffy rice.

super sushi rolls

This looks so impressive and yet it is easy and great fun to make. You will need to look for the ingredients in a good supermarket. Read the cooking instructions on the packet of sushi rice before you cook it, but my method below is how most sushi rice is cooked so it's likely to be similar.

SKILLS

cooking sushi rice • rolling up sushi • cutting

INGREDIENTS

To make about 30 pieces you need:

RICE

450 ml/2 cups water

225 g/1 generous cup Japanese rice for sushi

2 tablespoons rice wine vinegar

1 tablespoon golden caster/natural cane sugar

pinch salt

6 sheets nori seaweed

FILLINGS

ripe avocado strips and small, cooked prawns/shrimp OR smoked salmon and thin cucumber strips OR thin strips of omelette

You might like to eat your sushi with pickled ginger and soy sauce.

large saucepan • mixing bowl small bowl • spoon • sushi mat small paring knife

1 Put the water and rice into a large saucepan over medium heat on the hob/stovetop. Heat until the water comes to a boil (when the water is bubbling). Cover the pan with the lid, lower the heat and simmer for 10 minutes. Take the pan off the hob/stovetop and let stand for 15 minutes with the lid on. Spoon into a mixing bowl. In a small bowl, mix together the vinegar, sugar and salt. Pour the vinegar dressing over the rice, mix together and let cool.

2 Put a sheet of nori seaweed on a sushi mat. Use your hands or a spoon to cover two-thirds of the seaweed with rice. Leave a strip along the end of the seaweed furthest from you without rice. Press the rice down so that it is quite flat and evenly spread out.

3 Put a few strips of avocado and some prawns/shrimp along the middle.

4 Pick up the edge of the mat closest to you and roll up the seaweed and its filling into a big sausage. Use the mat to help you roll the seaweed neatly.

5 Squash the roll to make the sushi nice and compact, then unroll the mat. Do all this again with the remaining sheets of seaweed, rice and filling. Using the claw-cutting technique, cut each roll of sushi into 5 or 6 pieces with a small paring knife and serve with pickled ginger and soy sauce, if you like.

stuffed potato skins

Have you ever baked a potato before? A good baked potato should have a crisp skin and a light, fluffy middle. To achieve this you will need to bake them for an hour in a hot oven. My granny taught me to make these when I was little. Instead of instead of smoked haddock fillets, you can also try a few spoonfuls of tinned sweetcorn and handfuls of grated cheddar cheese – simply mix with the herbs, lemon and sour cream in step 4.

SKILLS

using scissors • baking potatoes • cooking fish
squeezing lemons • using oven • sharing

INGREDIENTS

For 4 people you need:

4 baking potatoes

3 smoked haddock fillets

a little unsalted butter

handful fresh herbs e.g. parsley or fennel tops

½ lemon

3 tablespoons sour cream or crème fraîche or a little butter

2 large handfuls baby spinach leaves, torn into small pieces

*fork • ovenproof dish • spoons • timer
oven mitts • scissors • mixing bowl
lemon juicer • table knife • clean napkin
roasting dish*

1 Turn the oven on to 190˚C (375˚F) Gas 5. Prick the potatoes all over with a fork.

2 Put the smoked haddock into an ovenproof dish and dot with a little butter using teaspoons.

3 Using oven mitts, put the potatoes as well as the haddock into the oven. Set a timer for 15 minutes. Using oven mitts, take the haddock out of the oven and put to one side. Set the timer for 45 minutes more for the potatoes.

4 Using scissors, snip the herbs into small pieces and put into a mixing bowl. Squeeze the lemon half over a lemon juicer and pour the juice over the herbs. Add the sour cream. When the fish is cool enough to handle, peel the flesh away from the skin and flake the fish into the bowl. Mix everything together with a fork.

5 Using oven mitts, take the potatoes out of the oven. Let cool slightly. Holding a potato with a clean napkin or oven mitt, use a table knife to cut the potato in half. Use a spoon to scoop the middle of the potato out of the potato skin and into the bowl with the haddock and herbs. Squash the chopped spinach into the potato skins. Mix the haddock mixture and cooked potato together in the bowl. Now spoon it back into the potato skins on top of the spinach. You will need to spoon the mixture between the potato skins. Using oven mitts, put the dish back in the oven and set the timer for another 10 minutes. Using oven mitts, take them out of the oven.

corn tortilla tubes

These are lots of fun to make and eat! The corn tortillas become lovely and crisp when you bake them in the oven. (You will need to use corn tortillas, not flour ones.) This is delicious with the Green Dip on page 30.

delicious with the Green Dip on page 30.

INGREDIENTS

To make 8 tubes you need:

1 red onion

1 garlic clove

3 carrots, well washed

1 tablespoon olive oil plus a little extra

500 g/1 lb. minced/ground beef or vegetarian equivalent

500 g/2 cups passata/tomato purée

pinch brown sugar

8 corn tortillas

salad and Green Dip (page 30), to serve

small paring knife • cutting board garlic press • grater • frying pan/skillet wooden spoon • ovenproof dish oven mitts

SKILLS

cutting • crushing garlic • frying rolling • using oven

1 Turn the oven on to 190˚C (375˚F) Gas 5. Peel the onion. Use the bridge-cutting technique to halve it with a paring knife. Using the claw-cutting technique, thinly slice it. Peel the garlic and crush it with a garlic press. Grate the carrots.

2 Put the oil, onion, garlic and carrots into a heavy-based frying pan/skillet over low heat on the hob/stovetop. Heat until soft.

3 Add the beef and fry for 10 minutes, or until it's turning golden brown. Add the passata/tomato purée and sugar, cover the pan with a lid, and cook gently for 10 minutes. The mixture will be quite dry, which is what you want.

4 Lay the tortillas on the cutting board and spoon some beef along the middle. Roll the tortillas around the beef and put into an ovenproof dish. Brush the tortilla tubes with a little oil. Using oven mitts, put the dish into the oven and cook for 15 minutes.

one-pot supper

This is a quick way to make a simple meal for your family to enjoy. To keep it really simple, you can put some baking potatoes into the oven to cook alongside. Use butter beans as an alternative to the chicken for a vegetarian option. This is also delicious with couscous (see page 62), rice (see page 101) or salad (see page 18).

SKILLS

garlic crushing • using scissors • using oven

INGREDIENTS

For 4 people you need:

185 g/1 cup pitted black olives

300 g/10 oz. roasted red (bell) peppers from a jar

2 sprigs fresh rosemary

2 tablespoons olive oil

400 g/14 oz. canned chopped tomatoes

2 garlic cloves

4 free-range chicken pieces e.g. thighs or legs, or 1 large jar or 2 tins butter beans, drained

baked potatoes, rice or mashed potatoes, or bread and salad, to serve

colander • scissors • mixing bowl garlic press • roasting dish • oven mitts

1 Turn the oven on to 180°C (350°F) Gas 4. Tip the olives (if they need draining) and roasted peppers into a colander over a mixing bowl to drain. Now pour the liquid out of the bowl.

2 Using scissors, snip the peppers into small pieces and put into the dry mixing bowl.

3 Add the rosemary, olive oil and tomatoes to the peppers, then squash the olives slightly to break them up and add to the bowl, too. Peel the garlic cloves and crush them with a garlic press. Add the crushed garlic to the bowl.

4 If using chicken, pull the skin off it with your fingers, throw the skin away, then add the chicken to the bowl. If using butter beans instead, add them to the bowl.

5 Mix everything with your hands to coat the chicken or beans in the pepper and olive mixture. Now WASH YOUR HANDS. Tip everything into a roasting dish. Using oven mitts, put the dish in the oven and cook for 35–45 minutes (depending on the size of the chicken pieces), or until the chicken is cooked all the way through – ask an adult to help you check this.

lemony & honey marinade

To make a marinade, you normally mix together an acid, like lemon juice or vinegar with an oil, like olive oil, sunflower oil or sesame oil. You then add some flavour with chopped herbs, spices or garlic. The marinade helps to keep the food juicy and stops it from drying out during cooking. You can also use a vegetarian meat replacement as an alternative to the chicken.

INGREDIENTS

For 4 people you need:

1 garlic clove

1 lemon

6 free-range skinless chicken thigh fillets, or a vegetarian meat replacement

2 tablespoons olive oil

2 teaspoons honey

1 teaspoon dried oregano

rolling pin • cutting board • lemon juicer small paring knife • mixing bowl spoon • roasting dish • oven mitts

SKILLS

bashing garlic • cutting • making marinade • squeezing lemons • using oven

1 Bash the garlic clove with a rolling pin – this will help to loosen the pink papery skin – then peel off the skin. Using the rolling pin again, squash the garlic to crush it slightly – this helps its flavour to come out as it cooks. Remember to wash the rolling pin after!

2 Use the bridge-cutting technique to halve the lemon with a small paring knife. Put a lemon half over a lemon juicer and press down to squeeze out the juice. Repeat with the other lemon half.

3 Put the chicken in a mixing bowl and add the garlic, lemon juice, oil, honey and dried oregano. Mix with a spoon, cover and put in the fridge for at least 1 hour. After 1 hour, turn the oven on to 190˚C (375˚F) Gas 5. Spoon the chicken into a roasting dish (leave the marinade behind). Using oven mitts, put the dish in the oven and roast for 25–30 minutes – ask an adult to help you check if it is cooked. Turn the chicken once during this time. Cut the chicken into small pieces to serve.

toffee apple tarts

These tarts are so enjoyable to make that the boys who came over to my house to make them for this book asked to make some more in between taking the photos. Once you know how to make pastry dough, you can make so many different pies, cheese straws, small tarts, big tarts and lots more.

SKILLS

cutting • rubbing butter into flour • lining tart tins/pans • sharing fillings • bashing with rolling pin • using oven

INGREDIENTS

To make 24 little tarts you need:

SWEET PASTRY/PIE CRUST DOUGH

115 g/1 stick unsalted butter, chilled

225 g/1¾ cups plain/all-purpose flour

1 teaspoon sugar

1 egg yolk (see page 84 for separating eggs)

1–2 tablespoons cold water

FILLING

about 6–8 eating apples

12 hard toffee sweets/candies

table knife • mixing bowl • clingfilm/plastic wrap • parchment paper 2 x 12-hole cupcake tins/pans rolling pin • cutting board • oven mitts round cutter about 8 cm/ 3 inches across

1 Use a table knife to cut the butter into small pieces and put into a mixing bowl with the flour. Rub the butter into the flour with your fingers until it looks like fine breadcrumbs. This can take a few minutes.

2 Add the sugar, egg yolk and water and stir the mixture together with the table knife until it comes together and you can form a ball with your hands. Wrap the pastry in clingfilm/plastic wrap and put it in the fridge for 30 minutes – this will make it easier to roll out.

3 Turn the oven on to 180˚C (350˚F) Gas 4. Using a scrap of parchment paper, rub a little butter inside the holes in the cupcake tins/pans. Break the dough into 4 pieces. Sprinkle a little flour on the work surface, then roll out one piece at a time. Dip the cutter in flour, then cut out 24 circles. Gently press the circles into the holes of the pans.

4 Use the table knife and a cutting board to cut the apples in small pieces, avoiding the core in the middle. Divide the pieces between the pastry cases/dough crusts.

5 Put the toffees on a solid work surface and GENTLY bash with the rolling pin to break into pieces. Scatter the pieces evenly over the apples. Using oven mitts, put the pans in the oven and bake for 15 minutes, or until the toffee has melted and the apples are cooked.

scones & jam

Make these once and you'll be making them on repeat. They're so good. Why not treat Mum and Dad and make them a batch at the weekend? You can also vary the flavour – see opposite for both sweet and savoury options.

SKILLS

rubbing butter into flour • cutting using cutters
brushing (milk) using pastry brush

INGREDIENTS

To make 8–10 scones you need:

225 g/1¾ cups self-raising/rising flour

1 teaspoon baking powder

40 g/2½ tablespoons unsalted butter, chilled

1 tablespoon sugar

140–150 ml/⅔ cup milk plus a little extra

strawberry jam, to serve

*scissors • parchment paper
baking tray • mixing bowl • table knife
round fluted cutter about 6 cm/2¼
inches across • pastry brush
oven mitts*

1 Turn the oven on to 220˚C (425˚F) Gas 7. Cut a piece of parchment paper big enough to cover the baking tray. Put the flour and baking powder into a mixing bowl. Use a table knife to cut the butter into small pieces and put into the mixing bowl with the flour. Rub the butter into the flour with your fingers until it looks like fine breadcrumbs. This can take a few minutes, so be patient and keep going!

2 Add the sugar and milk. Use a table knife to stir the mixture so it starts to come together.

3 Now use your hands to bring the mixture together to make a ball of dough.

OTHER GOOD THINGS TO ADD TO SCONES:

For fruit scones stir in 50 g/½ cup dried fruit, such as raisins or currants or chopped dried apple or apricots, when you add the sugar. Try adding a pinch of mixed spice/apple pie spice or cinnamon. For cheesy scones, leave out the sugar and stir in 50 g/½ cup grated hard cheese and chopped fresh herbs.

4 Sprinkle a little flour on the work surface, then tip the dough out of the bowl. Pat it gently to flatten until it is about 1.5 cm/ ⅔ inch thick. Dip the cutter in flour, then cut out scones from the dough. Put the scones onto the baking tray, spaced a little apart. Gather all the spare bits of dough together, roll together to make a ball and flatten out again. Cut out the rest of the scones – you should be able to make 8, 9 or 10 scones depending on the size of your cutter.

5 Dip a pastry brush into a little milk and brush over the scones. Using oven mitts, put the scones in the oven and bake for 10 minutes until risen and golden. Let cool slightly before cutting in half and serving with strawberry jam and cream, if you like it.

roasted fruit

When you bake fruit in the oven, the key is to not overcook it otherwise it will get too soft. The times will vary depending on the size of the fruit, but 15 minutes is good for large soft fruits like nectarines or peaches. If you choose smaller fruit like plums, cook them for just 10 minutes. Roasted fruits are great served with plain yogurt. For a treat, add half a teaspoon of thick cream to each fruit half before baking so that you have a sauce at the end of the cooking time.

INGREDIENTS

For 4 people you need:

4 peaches or nectarines, or 8 plums or apricots

3 tablespoons light brown sugar

capful almond or vanilla extract

30 g/2 tablespoons unsalted butter

cutting board • small paring knife spoon • ovenproof dish • oven mitts

SKILLS

cutting • coring/pitting fruit • using oven

1 Turn the oven on to 190°C (375°F) Gas 5. Use the bridge-cutting technique to cut the fruit in half: on a cutting board, make a 'bridge' with a thumb and finger of one hand and hold the fruit. Hold a small paring knife in your other hand and put the blade under the bridge, then cut downwards firmly. You will need to move the fruit around as you cut to avoid cutting through the stone. This will take a bit of time, patience and practice.

2 Use a teaspoon to scoop the stones out of the middle of the fruit. You might need to dig the spoon under the stone to take it out.

3 Rest the fruit in an ovenproof dish with the cut side facing up. Spoon the sugar evenly over each fruit half, add the almond extract and dot with little pieces of the butter. Using oven mitts, put the dish in the oven and bake for 15–20 minutes. I think these peaches look so beautiful, don't you?

magic citrus desserts

These desserts are light and fluffy on top, with a pool of lemon sauce at the bottom. They are delicate because of the egg white, and that's why they need to be cooked in a roasting dish with water around them to help them cook slowly.

SKILLS

grating • separating eggs • folding • whisking egg whites

INGREDIENTS

For 4–5 people you need:

1 unwaxed lemon and 1 unwaxed lime (or just 2 lemons or limes, if you like)

100 g/½ cup golden caster sugar/natural cane sugar

50 g/3½ tablespoons unsalted butter, soft

2 free-range eggs

75 g/½ cup plus 1 tablespoon self-raising/rising flour

250 ml/1 cup milk

small grater • mixing bowl
wooden spoon saucer • 2 bowls
balloon whisk • small paring knife
electric mixer • metal spoon • 4–5
small pudding basins • deep roasting
tin/pan • small jug/pitcher • oven mitts

1 Turn the oven on to 180°C (350°F) Gas 4. Using a small grater, grate the lemon and lime to make zest (see page 60) and put into a mixing bowl. Add the sugar and butter and mix well with a wooden spoon until it becomes fluffy and paler in colour. Crack an egg onto a saucer (see page 60), rest a small bowl over the yolk and tip the white into a clean bowl (see opposite). Add the egg yolk to the butter mixture in the mixing bowl and then repeat with the other egg.

2 Add the flour to the mixing bowl and, using a balloon whisk, mix together. Use the bridge-cutting technique to halve the zested lemon with a small paring knife. Squeeze the juice into the mixing bowl, add the milk and whisk.

3 Using a clean balloon whisk or an electric mixer (with help from an adult), whisk the eggs whites in their bowl until they are thick, white and make slight peaks.

4 Using a metal spoon, 'fold' the egg whites into the batter in the mixing bowl. 'Folding' means to carefully cut the batter and mix without beating all the air out of the egg whites. Fold until the whites are just mixed in.

5 Rub a little butter inside 4–5 small pudding basins and put them in a deep roasting tin/pan. Spoon the batter into the basins, then pour water from a small jug/pitcher into the roasting tin to come halfway up the sides of the basins. Ask an adult to help you put the tin in the oven using oven mitts. Bake for 35 minutes, or until the desserts are golden and cooked with a small pool of sauce in the bottom.

DID YOU KNOW?

The bowl for egg whites needs to be really clean, or you may not end up with fluffy egg whites.

blackberry pudding

This is as easy as 1, 2, 3. Measure the ingredients, mix them together and then bake. I have chosen to use ground almonds and single/light cream in this recipe for a really special dessert. However, if you don't have ground almonds you could use self-raising/rising flour and instead of cream you can use milk. It will not have the same flavour or texture, but it's still a nice dessert. You could also try to make this dessert with other fruits that are in season.

 SKILLS
melting butter • mixing • measuring • using oven

INGREDIENTS

For 4 people you need:

40 g/2½ tablespoons unsalted butter

3 free-range eggs

80 g/a scant ½ cup golden caster sugar/ natural cane sugar

capful vanilla extract

150 ml/⅔ cup single/light cream

100 g/1 cup ground almonds

350 g/2 baskets blackberries

a little sugar for the top

parchment paper • medium ovenproof dish • small saucepan • table knife jug/pitcher • fork • oven mitt

1 Turn the oven on to 180°C (350°F) Gas 4. Using a scrap of parchment paper, rub a little butter inside the ovenproof dish. Put the butter in a small saucepan over low heat on the hob/stovetop and heat gently until it has melted. Crack the eggs into a jug/pitcher (see page 60 for how to do this) and measure all the other ingredients.

2 Add the melted butter, sugar, vanilla extract, cream and ground almonds to the eggs in the jug/pitcher and mix together with a fork. Pour this batter into your ovenproof dish.

3 Dot the blackberries all over the batter. Using oven mitts, put the dish into the oven and bake for 30–35 minutes or until the pudding is cooked all the way through. It tastes great with ice cream or yogurt or on its own!

raspberry & white chocolate cake

This cake is based on the classic Victoria sponge cake with fresh raspberries and big white chocolate buttons for the top.

SKILLS

creaming butter & sugar
measuring • cracking eggs
folding flour • spreading
melting chocolate

INGREDIENTS

To make 1 big cake you need:

CAKE BASE

100 g/3½ oz. white chocolate

225 g/almost 2 sticks unsalted butter, soft

225 g/1 generous cup golden caster sugar/natural cane sugar

capful vanilla extract

4 eggs, at room temperature

225 g/1¾ cups self-raising/rising flour

400 g/14 oz. ripe raspberries (or fruits of the forest) plus extra to decorate

1 teaspoon baking powder

4 tablespoons raspberry jam

BUTTERCREAM

100 g/6½ tablespoons unsalted butter, soft

150 g/1 cup icing/confectioners' sugar

3 ripe raspberries

ICING

3 ripe raspberries

250 g/2 cups icing/confectioners' sugar

a little water

2 plates • parchment paper • spoon small saucepan • small heatproof bowl oven mitts • spoon • 2 x 20-cm/8-inch cake tins/pans • pencil scissors 3 mixing bowls • wooden spoon table knife • large metal spoon • fork

1 Cover a big plate with parchment paper. Half fill a small saucepan with water and sit a small heatproof bowl in the pan over the water (without the bowl touching the water). Break the chocolate into the small bowl. Put the pan over low heat on the hob/stovetop. When the water starts to heat up, the chocolate will melt. Don't touch the chocolate – leave it until it has melted. Turn the heat off and carefully, using oven mitts, take the bowl off the pan and stir the chocolate. Spoon circles of the chocolate onto the parchment paper and leave somewhere cold to set.

2 Turn the oven on to 180˚C (350˚F) Gas 4. Using a scrap of parchment paper, rub a little butter inside the cake tins/pans. Rest one tin on some parchment paper and draw around the tin with a pencil. Cut 2 circles out and put in the bottom of the tins.

3 Put the soft butter, sugar and vanilla extract in a mixing bowl and mix well with a wooden spoon until it becomes fluffy and paler in colour. Crack the eggs and add to the batter a little a time, mixing all the time. Add just a little flour, too.

4 Add the raspberries and gently mix together. Don't worry if the batter looks slightly lumpy or curdled – this is normal.

5 Add the flour and, using a large metal spoon, 'fold' it into the batter. 'Folding' means to carefully cut the batter and mix without beating all the air out of it.

6 Spoon the batter equally into the tins/pans. Using oven mitts, put the tins in the oven and bake for 20 minutes, or until the cakes are well risen and cooked through.

7 Using the oven mitts, take the cakes out of the oven. Let cool, then turn them out of the tins/pans and peel the paper off. To make the buttercream, put the butter, sugar and raspberries in a bowl and mix until really smooth. Put one of the cakes onto a plate and spread the jam over it. Spread the buttercream over the jam and put the other cake on top. To make the icing, mash the raspberries in a bowl with a fork, add the sugar and a little water and mix together. Spoon onto the cake and decorate with more raspberries and the white chocolate buttons.

raspberry & white chocolate cake 123

pick 'n' mix hot choc

For a really special hot chocolate, you can just melt chocolate into milk and then add flavour from orange zest or a spice. Otherwise, you can use sweetened cocoa mix. This is a great recipe for making when you have friends over. You can create your own 'drinks bar' with little bowls of spices or orange zest for flavour, and sweets/candies and chocolates for the top. Your friends are likely to have great fun choosing what to add to their hot chocolates.

SKILLS

measuring • pouring • grating

INGREDIENTS

To make 1 hot chocolate you need:

HOT CHOCOLATE

milk

a few squares milk chocolate or
2 teaspoons sweetened cocoa mix

FLAVOURING

freshly grated ginger, ground cinnamon,
grated orange zest

TOPPING

whipped cream in a can (or whipped
double/heavy cream)

a selection of sweets/candies e.g. white or
milk chocolate buttons, mini-marshmallows,
chocolate flakes, sprinkles

*cup • small saucepan
wooden spoon • spoon*

1 Measure the milk in the cup you will be using – pour the milk into your cup and then pour this milk into a small saucepan. Only three-quarters fill your cup, as you will need room for the toppings!

2 Add the chocolate to the pan and heat until it melts and the milk just starts to bubble – don't leave it too long otherwise the milk will rise up inside the pan and spill over the top! Take the pan off the heat. Stir with a wooden spoon until the chocolate has melted.

3 Pour the hot chocolate into your cup.

4 Now decide which flavour you would like to add to your hot chocolate – freshly grated ginger, ground cinnamon and grated orange zest are all good – and stir it in. Top the hot chocolate with whipped cream and chocolates and sprinkles. Why not add a flake, too?

index

conversion chart

Weights and measures have been rounded up or down slightly to make measuring easier.

Measuring butter:
A US stick of butter weighs 4 oz. which is approximately 115 g or 8 tablespoons.

American	Metric	Imperial
6 tbsp	85 g	3 oz.
7 tbsp	100 g	3½ oz.
1 stick	115 g	4 oz.

The recipes in this book require the following conversions:

Volume equivalents:

American	Metric	Imperial
1 teaspoon	5 ml	
1 tablespoon	15 ml	
¼ cup	60 ml	2 fl. oz.
⅓ cup	75 ml	2½ fl. oz.
½ cup	125 ml	4 fl. oz.
⅔ cup	150 ml	5 fl. oz. (¼ pint)
¾ cup	175 ml	6 fl. oz.
1 cup	250 ml	8 fl. oz.

Weight equivalents:

Imperial	Metric
1 oz.	30 g
2 oz.	55 g
3 oz.	85 g
3½ oz.	100 g
4 oz.	115 g
6 oz.	175 g
8 oz. (½ lb.)	225 g
9 oz.	250 g
10 oz.	280 g
12 oz.	350 g
13 oz.	375 g
14 oz.	400 g
15 oz.	425 g
16 oz. (1 lb.)	450 g

Measurements:

Inches	cm
¼ inch	5 mm
½ inch	1 cm
1 inch	2.5 cm
2 inches	5 cm
3 inches	7 cm
4 inches	10 cm
5 inches	12 cm
6 inches	15 cm
7 inches	18 cm
8 inches	20 cm
9 inches	23 cm
10 inches	25 cm
11 inches	28 cm
12 inches	30 cm

Oven temperatures:

120°C	(250°F)	Gas ½
140°C	(275°F)	Gas 1
150°C	(300°F)	Gas 2
170°C	(325°F)	Gas 3
180°C	(350°F)	Gas 4
190°C	(375°F)	Gas 5
200°C	(400°F)	Gas 6
220°C	(425°F)	Gas 7

acknowledgements

Thanks to everyone involved in this book, including Susan with gorgeous photos, the children with their amazing input, Iona with her lovely design, Penelope Leach with her helpful child psychology advice, and the late Marguerite Patten for her incredible foreword. Chatting with Marguerite in her home was a complete honour and a highlight of my career.